The Trees of Shropshire

The Trees of Shropshire

Myth, Fact and Legend

Andrew Morton

Drawings by Alan Howard
Photography by Tom Foxall, A.B.I.P.P.

Airlife
ENGLAND

Airlife Publishing Ltd.

7 St. John's Hill, Shrewsbury, England.

Contents

List of Illustrations

List of Plates

Foreword

Compared with most other European countries, Britain with 35 species, possesses a fairly limited variety of native trees and the selection seems even more spartan when compared with those of North America, China and Japan. What our native tree flora lacks in variety however, is amply compensated for by the rich history and folklore with which many of our living trees are associated.

Shropshire, as Andrew Morton points out, is particularly well endowed with old or otherwise remarkable trees, many of them situated in places one might best describe as a little off the "beaten track". If for no other reason therefore, this book should act as a spur to the exploration of one of England's least known and loveliest counties.

The trees and their histories however, form the real "meat" of this account and not surprisingly in this principally rural county, the churchyard yews and hedgerow oaks figure prominently. One of these, the Lydham Manor Oak, I remember visiting many years ago in the company of a Shropshire girl who later became my wife. It is thanks to my wife that I was first made aware of another famous Shropshire tree, the Arbor Tree at Aston-on-Clun. Her father, the late Charles Lloyd of Broome, was one of those charged with renewing the flags on this tree each year and on one occasion I was lucky enough to be asked to assist him. The tree, a pollarded black poplar, grows in the centre of the village by a bridge over the River Clun and I shall never forget climbing into its crown, there to receive the long larch poles onto which the new flags had been fixed.

Not far from Aston in the churchyard at Clun grows what is possibly Shropshire's oldest yew, a venerable specimen whose beginnings, according to one calculation, may have occurred 2000 years ago.

It is not just native trees however, that attract Mr. Morton. The parks, estates and gardens of the county boast an impressive tally of exotic trees of a large size and these too are given due mention in this fascinating account. The measurements made over many years by Alan Mitchell, Hatton Gardner and latterly Kim Dodwell and Andrew Morton himself are a valuable record of the more important trees of Shropshire and form a most useful appendix to the book.

Throughout the mass of historical detail we are constantly reminded of the author's love for Shropshire's trees and concern for their wellbeing. If future generations are to enjoy the beauty and lore of ancient trees we should do well to follow his lead.

Roy Lancaster

". . . Their shapes, their burrs and branch stumps and root-stocks are living records of what has happened to them historically. In their maturity trees are so etched with experience that they become recognizable not just as species but as individuals and then yet another kind of grain begins to develop – the accumulating layers of myth and affection that gather round ancient trees".

Richard Mabey (1980)

THE LADY OAK, CRESSAGE.

Introduction

What this book attempts to do is to look at individual trees in Shropshire; trees that have become unique either because of their size, or their age, or because of the history and legends associated with them. Shropshire is indeed fortunate in having many excellent trees growing on her fertile soils.

Historical records are sparse compared with other more populated counties, so there is much to be discovered by enquiry and research. Perhaps because of this sparseness of population many old and remarkable trees survive and are for the most part respected by their owners. However, the county of Shropshire still hides its treasures away largely unpublicised and unsung.

The richness, range and variety of Shropshire's trees assumes many surprising and interesting forms.

The ancient and mysterious yews, for example, are more numerous in Shropshire than in any other county. The relic oaks from the medieval forests maintain an historical link through widely differing centuries and times. The Arbor Tree with its flags is the country's last surviving relic of ancient tree dressing rites possibly from Celtic times. The combination of Europe's best tree house and Britain's largest lime make the Pitchford tree unique. Then there are the numerous great gardens and landed estates spread across the breadth of the county containing collections of magnificent specimen trees from the continents of the world.

This publication is not intended to be a field guide to species identification, nor is it a history of woodlands in Shropshire, although human influence on the early forests is briefly examined in the first chapter. In any case the existing woodlands and their distribution are well chronicled in the excellent publications of such organisations as the Shropshire Trust for Nature Conservation, the Nature Conservancy Council and the work of the C.P.R.E.; bodies which do so much to inform the public and landowners of the richness and vulnerability of Shropshire's diverse flora and fauna.

If this book succeeds in stimulating a more general interest in the county's trees, not just in the old and venerable trees, their history and mythology, but also in new plantings, it is hoped that a wider and deeper appreciation of the value and worth of trees will have been encouraged.

Andrew Morton
Shrewsbury, 1986.

Chapter 1
Woodland History

During the last ice age very few trees existed in Britain. Then in about 8000 BC the climate became warmer, the ice retreated northwards and most of Britain became clothed in trees. This huge forest covered the vast majority of the low-lying land and within it lived such large animals as the lynx, bear, beaver, reindeer, ox and wolf.

Our understanding of man's early exploits in this forest is very limited. The further we attempt to look back into prehistory the dimmer our knowledge becomes and it can be difficult to imagine the life of primitive man through our sophisticated 20th century eyes. Nevertheless, we can be reasonably certain that Mesolithic man created small clearings in the forest probably by deliberately setting fire to the trees.

One of the most significant steps in social evolution was from man the foodhunter to man the settled farmer and the first farming activity known to us in this country is from the Bronze Age when stone hoes were used to cultivate light soils in thin woodland. The early settlers' basic needs were water and land suitable for cultivation and, when felling trees, they used as much of the material as possible, converting the timber for shelters, the bark for food, fibres for ropes and threads, and leaves for fodder. They probably practised early woodland management, clearing trees to allow preferred species to flourish and when they had exhausted an area they moved on to start the process again.

The amazing hurdle trackways on the Somerset Levels, dating from around 3000 BC and the wooden henge monuments of the southern counties, are glorious testaments to the early use of timber with oak, ash, lime, hazel, alder and holly all in regular use. The sophistication of these structures indicates a great knowledge of trees and their timbers; trackways are the first real evidence of woodcraft in the world.

The composition of the virgin forest in 3000 BC has been roughly determined using the evidence of pollen deposits. The dominant species that existed then can still be traced in certain remnant woods today.

These dominant species are as follows:-

Area		
S.W. England and part of Norfolk	—	Lime
C. & E. Ireland, S.W. Wales, England	—	Elm and Hazel
S. Scotland, N. England, Wales	—	Oak and Hazel
W. Ireland		
N. Scotland	—	Pine and Birch

The wetter climate of the Bronze Age created bogs which altered and destroyed some areas of the forest. Man's persistent activities in the forest continued, probably on a far wider scale than we can imagine with the practice of coppicing (cutting back growth to a 'stool' that shoots again creating a renewable source of wood) used as a proper management regime. The Bronze Age travellers probably brought new species from mainland Europe and the great distances travelled by these early tradesmen should not be under-estimated. It is also worth remembering that social change was normally very gradual and conditions of human existence would remain essentially static for centuries only undergoing significant change whenever the effects of human invention or patterns of trade altered the economic basis of life.

By the time the Romans came to Britain it is sobering to think that the landscape of Britain was probably a relatively well managed one with established villages and farmsteads spread across the countryside. The basic framework, modified during the Roman occupation, was later to form the estate and parish boundaries of the late Saxon period. The Celtic peoples who inhabited late Iron Age Britain had a distinctive culture and one that developed independently from their origins on mainland Europe. Fragments of this culture survive today, for example, their magical feast 'Samain' held on the Celtic New Year of 1st November when it was neither the old year nor the new — we now call Hallowe'en. 'Beltane', on 1st May, was a fertility celebration surviving in fragile form today as the May Queen Festival. During these Celtic times wood was used for many purposes from intricate hurdlework and basketry to cooking utensils. The Iron Age carpenter became a skilled craftsman.

The arrival of the Romans (AD 40) brought intense new activity with many of their constructions being of timber, notably the Roman forts. Existing coppices were maintained in order to fuel Roman baths, furnaces and kilns; much new land was cleared for agriculture. The population at the height of the Roman occupation was probably in excess of 1 million, though it must be remembered that Britain was at the edge of the Roman Empire and away from the south east, the effect of the Romans on the rural population was probably minimal with life and beliefs continuing much as before.

After the Romans left, life in the Dark Ages is little recorded. There was inter-tribal rivalry and fighting, but the popular concept of the Anglo-Saxon barbaric destruction of Britain and the subsequent setting up of the village pattern appears from recent research to be a myth. It seems more likely that the invasion was gradual and less violent; newcomers very often settled alongside the established inhabitants and it was the later migrants who colonised and cleared areas of the still extensive woodland cover. The Saxons set up their own administration and later in this period the common language of the people became an early form of English. The Saxon palaces, such as those in Northumberland and Somerset, show a high degree of developed design and woodwork skill and some Anglo-Saxon church doors are still in use today, over 1,000 years after their construction. The Saxon land charters list boundary trees with reference to many species such as yew, pear, apple, maple, thorn and pollard oaks. Here there is written evidence of individual trees in the landscape assuming some importance.

From the early English language can be found references to what was happening in the landscape, a classic example being the word 'leah' now 'ley' meaning a permanent glade or clearing in the forest and the many place names ending in 'ley' such as Dawley, Madeley, Billingsley and Glazeley, show us how those settlements came into being. From about 800 AD the population increased and agriculture became more organised with the church and Saxon nobility having firmer control, especially in the south and east.

The centuries after the Norman invasion in 1066 to about 1300 saw more village establishment as the population dramatically increased to 5 million. Each village had its own church and manor house, and the local lord of the manor had hunting grounds nearby each village. By about 1400 nearly all the villages that exist today had been created, but around 25% of them had become deserted by the late Middle Ages when the population began to decrease.

Just how much the native forest was modified during the eleven centuries between the Iron Age and the Norman invasion is difficult to ascertain. We know that in parts of southern and eastern England the forest cover was almost completely altered; in the west and north the process was far slower. But by about 1250 it is doubtful whether any significant areas of woodland in England had been left untouched. In Scotland and Ireland virgin forest probably remained intact until the 17th century. In these times the classic English lowland landscape of woodlands surrounded by farmland came into being with the main function of the woodland being to produce 'underwood' for burning and fencing and timber for building purposes. The medieval landscape became what it was due to intricate management methods and strict laws with over one third of the country under Royal Forest Law. (This meant the King had the hunting rights.) These Forest Laws not only covered woodland areas but also wastes and moorland. Outside the Royal Forests the trees of the land belonged to the lords of the manor, while villagers took deadwood and underwood and had some rights to timber for repairs. The use of woodlands as pasture (wood pasture) prevented regeneration, but with the 'pollarding' of individual trees (cutting off limbs of trees above the reach of animals), a regular supply of fresh branches made pollarding a popular management practice. By the 13th century the universal system of woodland management was coppicing and wood pasture. Complicated laws existed with even the lords of the manor sometimes unable to fell trees so as to ensure a regular supply of wood remained available for the whole population.

Although the art of coppicing remained and the practice continued into this century, by the 1890s it was in serious decline. The First and Second World Wars were responsible for great losses of timber. The remaining woods were largely replaced by coniferous plantations and the use, since the Second World War, of large mechanical equipment that can easily 'grub out' old coppice stools has dramatically increased the destruction of old woodland.

It is also worth mentioning that the parks, still such a feature of the English landscape, were originally a medieval creation, with the production of venison as the first priority. The individual parkland trees were usually pollarded and some of these early parks survive in various places, e.g., Moccas Park in Herefordshire. The continuity of the park in the landscape culminated in the great 18th century landscaped parks with 'Capability' Brown and Humphrey Repton, two of the most famous exponents.

It can be seen then, that from the mists of prehistoric times until present day the use made of the woodlands and their produce has had a great influence on the appearance of the landscape. We see today that trees and their timber have never been far away from everyday life.

Chapter 2
History of Shropshire Forests

Settlements in Shropshire can be dated from within the Bronze Age period (around 2500 BC). Burials at Bromfield near Ludlow, the Clun-Clee ridgeway (an early trading route), tumuli on the Long Mynd and boats recovered from the meres in the north of the county are all testimony to early activity. From a later period come the Iron Age hill forts which are such an outstanding feature of the high places in the county. Apart from high ground and the marsh lands of the north most of the land we now call Shropshire would have been densely wooded during the Roman occupation and through into the Saxon period (AD 400).

It has already been stated that the basic framework of the landscape owes much to Celtic pre-Christian influences and Rowley states that places in the west, such as Clun, may well have been uninterrupted settlement sites from very early times. Place names can give clues to the history of an area and the continuing existence of such Celtic names as Severn, Lawley, Clee, Caer Caradoc clearly show their early origins.

Early written evidence of the use of timber can be taken from the account of the building of Watling Street by the Romans. "The road was built upon oak and holly logs laid obliquely upon the clay subsoil." The Roman City of Viroconium "White town by the Alders," gives further reference to trees.

Not much is known of the Dark Ages in Shropshire, but we know that the arrival of the Saxons hastened woodland clearance. By the 9th century AD this colonisation seems to have accelerated.

From 1005 the Anglo-Saxon Mercian shires had an administrative identity of their own and Shropshire became the first to be named. The regional capital was and still is Shrewsbury and the old name "Scrobbesbyrig" described the town and the county.

In 1086 the well-known Norman Domesday survey gave a valuable glimpse of what was happening in those times, although it was not totally comprehensive, in this the mention of 'hayes', medieval animal parks, mainly for deer were recorded regularly over the county with over 60 being named in Shropshire. These small hunting areas were found either in or at the edge of woodland and they were usually enclosed by a hedge, wall or fence. Some of these hayes survived in different forms into the Middle Ages.

During the medieval period considerable areas of Shropshire were designated "Royal Forests" under the general administrative heading of the "Shropshire Forest". At their peak over 50 per cent of the county was covered by the forest law. Forest not only meant wooded areas but also scrub land and heath land, a local example being the Clee and Clun Forest areas. The sheer size of these forest areas made administration very difficult.

The Royal Forests of Shropshire were gradually eroded away during the 13th and 14th centuries, but some of the woodlands became incorporated into landed estates and parks. The process of clearing woodland for pasture was often done on a large scale by the monasteries such as the Cistercian establishment of

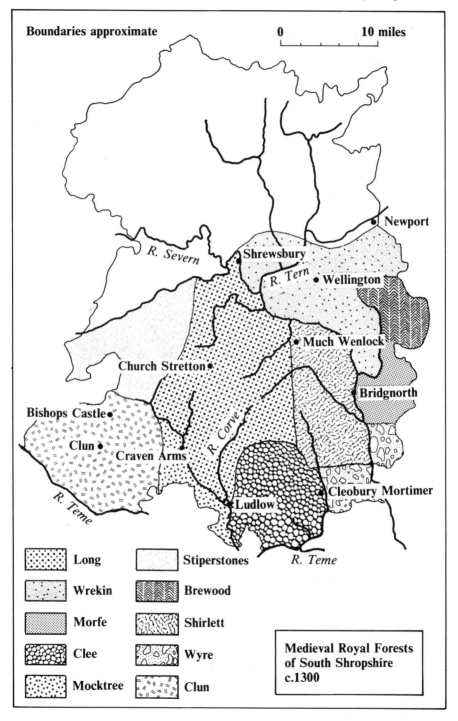

Boundaries approximate

0   10 miles

Newport

R. Severn

Shrewsbury

R. Tern   Wellington

Much Wenlock

Church Stretton

Bridgnorth

Bishops Castle

Clun

R. Corve

Craven Arms

Cleobury Mortimer

R. Teme

Ludlow

R. Teme

Long		Stiperstones		
Wrekin		Brewood		
Morfe		Shirlett		
Clee		Wyre		
Mocktree		Clun		

**Medieval Royal Forests
of South Shropshire
c.1300**

Buildwas and the Augustinians of Haughmond and Lilleshall. These monasteries during their heyday controlled and managed much land, including woodland, pasture and arable land.

LOCATION OF ROYAL SHROPSHIRE FORESTS

Long Forest
A very large forest stretching from Meole Brace to Sutton down the Severn to Cressage and Much Wenlock, south west to Craven Arms around the Long Mynd to Wentnor and through Longden back to Meole Brace.

Clee Forest
Included the Brown Clee, Ditton Priors and Culmington. It was approximately 2400 acres and ceased as a Royal Forest in 1155, but continued as a private estate. Much of this forest was open country.

Mt. St. Gilbert (Wrekin) Forest
Adjoined the Long and Shirlett Forests, included Hadnall, Astley, Roden, Wrockwardine, Crudgington, Shifnal, Uffington and then north of Shrewsbury to Albrighton.

Shirlett
Between the Long and the Clee it remained partly under Royal control until the 16th century. A small area remains around the Shirlett area of the Willey estate. The ridges around Monkhopton and Acton Round were part of this forest.

Morfe
Approximately eight miles by six and was sometimes referred to as the Bridgnorth Forest, predominately growing on the red sandstone to the east of the Severn. This forest originally joined the Wyre in the south.

Stiperstones (Hockeston)
To the north of Stiperstones and taking in Lords Hill.

A view of Saxton's map of 1577 shows that as late as the end of the 16th century large areas of tree-covered land still existed. In the north east Kings wood, south of Newport, describes by name who owned the land. Further north, around Hinstock, there was still thick woodland cover. Also in the north west the area around Whittington called Babbinswood Forest and in the extreme south, Mocktree Forest, were still large enough pieces of land to have forest identity.

Chapter 3
Tree Mythology

"The groves were God's first temples" — Bryant

Trees and Religion

The felling and clearance of trees to make way for agriculture, and therefore the expansion and progress of human civilisation, is an activity which has gone on practically uninterrupted for thousands of years and is still continuing in many parts of the world.

In one sense, because the tree or rather the wild forest has always stood in the way of progress, it might appear that mankind has little regard for such natural objects.

Paradoxically, this is very far from the truth and whilst man has seemingly striven in recent times to tame nature, in earlier times trees have had a peculiarly dominant influence on both human life and the human imagination.

Civilisation has, over many centuries, literally emerged from the wildwood and it is clear that trees, as well as supplying basic needs, have deeply affected human spiritual development. This is not an extravagant claim, and if it now appears so, it is only because we are now, compared to our forebears, more alienated and divorced from the land and the natural world.

For primitive man living constantly within a dense, virtually trackless forest, full of real and imagined terrors, trees, according to Sir James Frazer, have been one of the primary motivating forces in the evolution of religion, second only to the fear of the human dead.

Given the very short and erratic human life span, trees must have seemed immortal, especially the evergreens, which remained throughout the year apparently unchanged and unaffected by the natural cycle of the seasons upon which survival depended. The yearly miracle of germination, growth, fruition and rebirth must have seemed like an eternal battle between life and death, especially so in the climate of the Near East, the so-called 'cradle of civilisation'.

How strong, before the Roman invasion, the influences and echoes of that distant civilisation were in Britain is very difficult to say. Unfortunately for us, much of the research into history and ancient folklore has been directed at that favoured region fringing on the Mediterranean rather than Britain. Even the best descriptions of the Celts and their priests the Druids have come down to us from Roman writers such as Pliny the Elder and Julius Caesar, who were writing, it should be remembered for Roman readers.

Before the Romans, the spread of cultural influences in any densely forested island such as Britain would have been heavily dependent upon sea and river access and Britain did not have for example the inland navigational equivalent of the German Rhine.

Nevertheless there is abundant evidence to prove that from time immemorial trees have, all over the world, been the subject of intense religious veneration. From the first glimmerings of intelligence there has plainly been an urgent human need to make sense of the seemingly hostile natural world. Given this need for answers to the large questions of life and the ever present tendency to translate reality into mythic imagery the tree became identified with God or at least it was imagined to embody a deity. Therefore some trees were singled out for special reverence, and it appears that whilst there are continental, even regional differences in tree worship, there are also many world wide similarities. Comparisons with 'primitive' or isolated societies often provide valuable insights as without external pressure traditions die hard and slowly. Britain, particularly the Western areas, displays such tendencies to a degree.

First came the veneration, fear and reverence for the tree itself. The image of a great tree with its roots far into the underworld with a pillar-like trunk containing blood-like sap and with its branches reaching into the heavens became embedded in the human consciousness from very early times. In Mesopotamia the cedar was both deity and oracle. The tree as 'oracle' or the tree of knowledge is mentioned many times in the Old Testament and examples are recorded from Armenia, Arabia and Persia. There was a prophetic grove of evergreen oaks on Eventine Hill in Rome and tree omens were important to Romans; for example the withering of laurels, which foretold Nero's death. The Scythians practised divination with willow rods and the Druids used 'omen sticks' perhaps of fruit branches. Such wands and rods were forerunners of sceptres, heralds' wands and generals' staffs, all being symbols of power derived from the original sacredness of the tree. The tree as oracle was thought to be connected through its roots to wisdom and foreknowledge of the dead. The tree of life is an equally persistent idea found in many parts of the world.

Tree worship was obviously well established by the time of the first known representations and sacred trees appear on Chaldean and Assyrian engraved cylinders and on temples. The concept of the tree as God's dwelling place appears in both Egyptian and Persian mythology, where the cypress is considered especially sacred. Tree worship was also widespread in India. To Buddhists the bo-tree *(Ficus religiosa)* is regarded as the shrine tree. This extraordinary tree can be found in the grounds of Buddhist temples and where it grows shrines are often constructed. The incredible age of these trees have over the centuries reinforced their sanctity. The greatest of the bo-trees, "the Maha-bodhi tree of Anvradhapura" in Sri Lanka can be traced back to 245 B.C. The tree was grown from a branch brought to Sri Lanka from the original tree at Buddha Gaya on the Northern reaches of the Ganges in India. Under the original tree Buddha attained enlightenment. From that tree cuttings were taken to many places, including the royal park at Anvradhapura. The branch was planted in a special enclosure to mark the King of Ceylon's conversion to Buddhism. The event is recorded in detail in the Mahavamsa, the great historical chronicle of Sri Lanka. The tree still lives, the old shell gone, but the great growth from the original root and branch are still to be seen making it the oldest recorded living tree on earth. The bristle cone pines, the redwoods, the cedars of Lebanon, the cypresses of the Holy Land, the beobabs of Africa and some of the British yews could be of greater age, but none can match such a continuous and well documented historical record.

In Greece and Rome personified deities abounded. In both countries Gods were worshipped in connection with both individual trees and groves. Artemis the Moon Goddess was in different places Goddess of the Cedar, Hazel, Laurel, Myrtle and Willow. The chief God of Rome, in the form of Jupiter Feretrius appears to have been a sacred tree, probably an oak, and Rome was reputedly founded where the floating cradle of Romulus and Remus became entangled in the roots of a fig tree *(Ficus ruminalis).*

In so many ways the pervasive influences of the ancient Near East seem impossible to ignore and tree mythology is no exception. As revealed in ancient literature and folklore the age-old memory of the sacred groves is both intriguing and revealing, providing a key to some of the more puzzling remnant practices associated with trees and vegetation which still linger on today in many places, including Britain.

Sacred groves were, as Frazer demonstrates with great profundity, seats of ancient rural power. It was in these sacred groves of oak, in classical antiquity, that religious rites were performed and where priestly and kingly power was transferred, sometimes by bloody battle. They were it appears the forerunners of parliament and church before power finally moved to urban centres. A notable sacred grove of oaks was that of Zeus at Dodena which flourished it is said for over 2,000 years, but the archetypal grove on which Frazer centres his attention after long and involved investigation is the sacred grove of the goddess Diana at Nemi. In the heady language of classical mythology it is said that 'the priest-king who served the oak goddess Diana in her sacred grove bore the name Rex Nemorensis, the 'King of the Wood'. This sinister being stalked the grove and remained in power until he was challenged and killed in personal battle'.

'The challenger had first to break off a bough of the sacred oak — the 'Golden Bough' thus proclaiming his challenge'. 'The King of the Wood' was a personification of the oak god Jupiter. This priest King was originally named Virbius (the Green one). The sacred union of Virbius and Diana was 'intended to make the earth gay with the blossom of Spring and with the fruits of Autumn and to gladden the hearts of men and women with healthful offspring'.

Frazer also identifies the Golden Bough with the mistletoe which ancient peoples believed to be the god-presence in the tree.

Trees and Fertility

There is a closely related and widespread mythology concerning tree spirits and vegetation spirits, much of it being imitative magic, concerned with attempts to make corn grow. It is obvious that agriculture has had, as well as tree worship, a tremendous influence on religion. Examples include the custom of the Harvest-May still observed by some peasant peoples of Europe, where a large branch of hawthorn is brought back with the last sheaf of corn. This represented the spirit of vegetation on which depended next year's harvest.

It is said that it is from these primitive beliefs in vegetation spirits that the custom of the Maypole originates.

In Britain and Europe the Maypole, a standing trunk, was worshipped as a fertility symbol of the vegetation god, this recognised practice continuing into the 17th century. A Puritan commentator, Stubbs, described the Maypole as 'a stinking idol' and labelled the local population leaping and dancing around it 'heathens dedicating their idolles.' The still present custom of the May Queen is a persistent practice which preserves the folk-memory of a sacred marriage to promote fertility of the land. Frazer strongly hints that this King and Queen of May are the last surviving remnants of the legend of Virbius and Diana of Nemi. The Long Parliament of 1644 forbad the Maypole and though it came back after the Restoration, leaping and dancing were never quite the same again. Worship apparently of the tree trunk occurs in India where Hindu women praying for long life for their husbands wind cotton threads around a banyan tree whilst sitting in a circle around it. Speculative comparisons with the weaving of ribbons around the Maypole are inescapable.

Early rituals including tree rituals were often intended to ensure fertility and little distinction was made between human fertility and the fertility of the earth, perhaps a reflection of the oneness of man and nature.

Jack O'Green in popular belief is the sacrificial figure of the old woodland spirit who is killed off by the new spirit of Spring and the new growth. No doubt in a more primitive past a victim was sacrificed before the ceremony became ritualised. The whole complicated ceremony of the Green Man and the May Day observances include the choice of a King or Queen of May almost always finally symbolically sacrificed and who is typically clothed in oak leaves.

But what remains? On the surface not a great deal. Interpreting the meaning of remnant practices and fragments of folklore memory is difficult and confusing. Much of the history of such things was branded pagan by the Puritans and later the Victorians literally rewrote many old stories and suppressed what they regarded as unacceptable to Christianity and good taste.

Nevertheless some things remain still. The face of the mythical Jack, partly hidden by oak leaves, can be found in medieval churches in the region; some particularly good effigies in wood, stone and glass can be seen in the Parish Church of St. Mary's, Nantwich, Cheshire. At Knutsford in Cheshire on May Day, Green Jack still leads the carnival procession.

In Britain, Vernemeton 'the especially sacred grove' is recorded in Nottinghamshire in Roman times and Medionemeton 'the Middle Sanctuary' is thought to have been located at Cainpapple near Antoine Wall in Scotland. There are sacred groves recorded in Anglesey where the Druids made their last refuge from the Romans.

There is ample evidence from the literature of the Celtic world about the use of single sacred trees and groves as the gathering points for tribal and ritual assembly. These sacred precincts or 'temenoi' would have consisted of a sacred tree frequently associated with a venerated well near which a shrine would be constructed using temporary materials such as wood or wickerwork, sometimes stone, on which objects and idols were displayed to the people who assembled for the various seasonal festivals.

An early Irish tradition refers to the revered Omna 'oak' and the sacred tree of

Mugna was a yew, *(Eo Mugna)*. The tree of Ross *(Eo Rosa)* was also a yew. Other Irish sacred trees were Tortu's tree, an ash, and the tree of Dath-I, also an ash. Assemblies were held under these trees and it was sacrilegious to damage them in any way.

According to Laing[1] most places sacred to the Celts were unmarked by structures so that nothing remains of these natural sacred places except the very occasional remains of a wooden temple,[2] invariably built of oak. With the Celts as with other peoples certain trees and groves of trees *(nementi)* were held sacred and treated with great veneration. The Druids, the Celtic priests, chose groves of oak for the sake of the tree alone and never performed a sacred rite without having a branch of it.[3] Boughs of oak were found in an oak coffin in a tumulus at Gristhorpe in 1834 where mistletoe was also found. The Druids thought that anything that grew on an oak tree had been sent by God himself.

The early Christian missionaries found that they had to contend in Britain as in ancient Germany with the sacred grove, trying to destroy them or build their churches within them in order to subvert their power.

Tree sanctuaries
A holy tree might also afford the right of asylum. There are many classical allusions to tree sanctuaries such as the holy tree at Ephesus where the Amazons found refuge. Orestes fleeing from the Furies found safety under Apollo's laurel whilst at Phlius in the Pelopennese in a sacred cypress grove, fugitives found refuge from the normal course of justice and the trees were festooned with prisoners' discarded chains.

Perhaps the practice of building tree houses is an expression of the tree as a place of sanctuary.

Tree dressing
In its earliest form tree dressing is a form of stylisation of a worshipped, sacred tree and was accomplished by placing on the tree a mask or cloak to represent the god. Paucanius, 2nd century A.D., records the cult of the hanging Artemis in Arcadia presumably in reference to a mask hung on a sacred tree. Artemis along with Diana were Greek and Roman Moon Goddesses who in much earlier times ruled over the activity of hunting. The moon was for ancient peoples a female symbol of fertility and myths around a Goddess of the Moon grew in many cultures well before Greek and Roman times.

The root cause of this connection is thought to lie in the supposed ancient belief that the waxing and waning of the moon was related to female menstrual cycles and also to the monthly night hunting expedition at the time of the full moon and the unlicensed celebrations thereafter.

Be that as it may, throughout Eastern countries there was the practice and there still is here and there, of hanging gifts on any particular sacred tree, or attaching pieces of clothing to it so that luck, good health and fertility would attend the wearer. In the Himalayas wooden constructions are to be found at cross-roads and have been seen in recent times.

Maximus of Tyre, writing during the 2nd century A.D., refers to the

[1]Celtic Britain
[2]Heathrow and S. Cadbury
[3]Pliny the Elder

continuing worship of individual trees notably during the festival of Dionysus when anyone with a tree in their garden dressed it up to represent the god. In Greece and Rome sacred trees received the trophies of the chase and the arms of the conqueror.

Trees, pillars and standing stones

Although the original object of veneration was the tree itself and still is in some primitive tribes, growing sophistication over time produced change and stylisation. Symbolic representation of the original form or practice usually occurred and it is found that an erect tree trunk form eventually took the place of actual trees.

Altars might be placed either before the tree or the erect trunk for offerings. The next step was to transform the trunk into a pillar of stone, the advantage of this being that a pillar could be erected at any desired spot.

Sir Julian Huxley[1] describes the obelisk temple at Byblos as 'a savage forest of primitive stone pillars'. A further stage is the carving of the trunk into a statue to personify a deity.

The pillars of Greek temples were probably representations of tree trunks in that they have stylised foliage at the top. It is thought that the Greek temple is a formalised architectural version of the sacred grove.

Sacred stone circles would originally have been built in woodland clearings and were, it is thought, to have been preceded by circles of erect tree trunks as in the Wiltshire Woodhenge. The circle, a symbol of the cosmos, was itself an abstract sacred sign to early man. Natural circles in a world devoid of precise man-made geometry, were a rarity; there was the sun, the full moon and little else.

Ancient religious sites, based upon the magic cult are therefore invariably round. Within is the sacred, without is the profane. The circles were constructed by various means, by ditches, by mounds, by standing timbers and by standing stones and were demarcated by evergreen trees, in Britain normally the yew. In recent times circles have been reinforced by stone walling in many places. The fringing of sacred sites by planted trees is reminiscent of the sacred grove which was presumably achieved by felling and clearance or occurred naturally.

*Lady Oak
of Cressage*

[1]From an Antique Land

Chapter 4
Yews

This solitary tree. A living thing
Produced too slowly ever to decay
of form and aspect too magnificent
to be destroyed.
                        Wordsworth.

The oldest and most mysterious trees of the British Isles are the churchyard yews. It is safe to assume that typical large yews with huge trunks, often hollow, and growing in those churchyards which are known to be early religious sites, are the most ancient living things in Britain. These extremely old trees are mainly located in the south and west of these islands with a few specimens in the Midlands, the North West and Scotland. Surprisingly the largest in Britain is found at Fortingall in Scotland, this being considerably greater in girth (at 50ft) than any other British yew.

In Shropshire we have probably more ancient yews than any other county in Britain. The Shropshire trees follow the natural pattern of distribution with the

Uppington Yew – with the Roman altar in front of the tree.

majority located in the south and west of the county. Much work is at present being carried out on the dating and growth rates of yew trees using modern scientific methods of age determination and by the thorough researching of historical records. Over the next few years we should have a clearer picture as to how long some individual trees have been growing on their sites and a better understanding of the yew's longevity. This is intriguing work, for not only does it promise to yield valuable facts related to tree history, but it may also aid churchyard archaeological work. The indications are that some 12th century churches in particular may well have yew trees growing in close proximity which pre-date them. This reinforces other strong evidence that such sites were used for religious purposes in much earlier times, that is in the Anglo-Saxon, the Celtic period or even earlier.

The fact that many of the southern Shropshire churchyards have a characteristic raised circular shape indicates probable extreme age, certainly a pre-Christian origin. In Wales some churchyards are located not only on known Celtic enclosures but stand within the banks of prehistoric circles with the standing stones still remaining. A good example of this is Gwytherin in North Wales where four standing stones can still be seen within the mounded churchyard, one of them converted to use as a tombstone in the 5th century. Predictably, on this site are several massive yew trees.

Old religious sites are commonly located in close proximity to water whether a stream, well or spring. Hope Bagot churchyard has a spring which issues from below the roots of the clearly ancient churchyard yew.

What remains a mystery is the direct historical relationship of the yew tree with worship. Popular legend says that yews were simply planted to supply suitable wood for long bows and, although this may have some truth in later centuries, the key to the religious significance of the yew obviously lies in much earlier times. Very little documentary evidence exists. We do know that the name, yew, is Celtic and that this is the only tree which has retained its Celtic name.

We know also that in AD 597, when St. Augustine was sent to Britain, he was instructed not to destroy the temples of pagan Britain, but to establish Christian churches on these sites in order to successfully convert the native British to Christianity. At the Councils of Auxerne (AD 578), Tours (AD 637) and Nantes (AD 658) the practice of tree worship *(cultus arborum)* was forbidden.

Probably the evergreen yew was a symbol of immortality, never losing its leaves in winter and apparently living for ever.

Vaughan Cornish, the historian, suggested in 1947 that the yew may well have been a holy tree in Britain before Druidical times and was merely adopted by the Druids.

In these early times evergreen species were very few, only juniper, holly and yew being clothed in green in the winter months. It is significant that the holly also has many myths and legends associated with it. This 'rarity value' of the three indigenous British evergreens remained until the systematic introduction of foreign plants from other countries began in the 17th century. In Mediterranean countries the evergreen cypress, which also lives to a great age, is planted in graveyards.

The Roman scholar, Pliny the Elder, wrote of the Druids and their veneration

Clun Yew – of great age but with the original trunk decayed, new growth gives the tree a healthy crown.

of the oak; there is no mention of the yew. Here it must be remembered that, like Julius Caesar, Pliny was addressing Romans for whom the oak was a personification of Jupiter, their chief God. Like Julius Caesar, he may have been indulging in inadvertent praise. Nevertheless, considering the obvious importance of the yew in our ancient culture, the omission is curious.

There is a great deal of evidence to show that the Celts of Britain pursued and developed their own culture in relative isolation from the rest of Europe and it is, therefore, very difficult to say to what extent their religious and cultural attitude to trees was affected by classical Mediterranean example. Island Britain was a place where traditions persisted and died very slowly. It was the cultural backwater of Europe and at the very edge of classical influence.

It is in Wales where the yew has its strongest association with religion and here it is known that the yew was a consecrated tree *(Cambrian Register)*. It also appears that it was only in Britain, Ireland and Northern France, that the yew was considered a holy tree, although it is known that there were early pre-Celtic influences on Wales from the Iberian peninsular where the yew is common. No definite historical connection though has been established.

It would appear that the yew has been planted on religious sites right up until recent times and a customary tradition seems to have developed obscuring the original purpose. These sacred burial sites were also festival sites and were, in addition, a focus for community activities.

It may be that the sense of immortality created by the tree, the intense gloom spread by its evergreen crown, combined with more practical reasons such as the natural shelter it affords against the elements, made it a natural choice as possibly the earliest holy shelter; a suitable place for preaching or the practice of religious rites. At Nant Glynn, near Denbigh, even today can be seen an ancient yew containing stone steps and a pulpit built into the hollow trunk for outdoor services. In Normandy there is an enormous hollow yew which houses a tiny chapel.

The development of holy shelters into chapels and churches is characterised by the use of wood, first to provide the main structure and then by its use as an internal roof support and to provide pews, panelling and screens. It is hard not to see in the medieval churches and cathedrals the resemblance to the yew in the characteristic fluting and spreading pillars.

In Ireland the yew was once plentiful in association with sacred places. The pre-Christian religion of Ireland was Druidical and in AD 1158 Prince John's historian, Gerald de Barri (known as Giraldus Cambrensis, wrote in *Topographia Hybernica,* "compared with all other countries which we have entered here the yew abounds especially in ancient cemeteries and places sacred to Saints, planted of old for decoration and ornament and now we see many of them broken down and trampled". The trees referred to must have been old when de Barri wrote those words. In some parts of Ireland and Britain the yew is still referred to as the palm from when the tree's foliage was used on Palm Sunday because the true palm was not available in the British Isles. Up until last century in some districts of Britain yew foliage was placed in coffins at burials so as to ensure immortality.

The Shropshire Yews

The view that some existing yew trees in Shropshire churchyards could be over 1,000 years old and possibly much older, is not shared by everybody, nor is it a new statement. Legends speak of very old trees, the yews in Ashford Carbonel churchyard are by local tradition said to be 1,500 years old. The great yew tree at Church Preen is talked of as being over 1,000 years old. Writers, particularly in the Victorian era, liked the idea of ancient trees. They also claimed that oaks, as well as yews, were of great age and any tree was tagged ancient if it had a girth of over 6 metres (20 feet). Their views on the age of other species were usually wildly off target, but the romantic idea that some trees can live to be thousands of years old seems only achievable by the yew. The yew tree must be considered separately from all other British tree species where age is concerned. Some yews measured a hundred years ago have hardly shown any increase in girth measurement over that time. How long have they remained in that state, hardly growing at all? How long has a tree been growing that measures 9 metres (30 feet) in circumference and which, two hundred years ago, measured 8.5 metres (28 feet)?

It is tempting to believe it can be calculated, but there are many other variable factors as well as girth to be taken into account. In its early life the yew can grow fairly vigorously and has, on occasions, achieved 3.5 metres (12 feet) girth in 200 years. It seems that from then on it slows down appreciably and can almost appear to stop growing. It also has the ability to rejuvenate itself with new growth from inside and outside the old trunk. This initial process to maturity can take several hundred years. In Eastham churchyard on the Wirral stands a yew that was written about as being an old tree in 1150. The tree fits the description in the parish records, and has fresh growth from the old decayed base. It looks as if it could happily continue to exist if left undisturbed for many centuries to come. The Eastham yew is exceptional in that it was written about in 1150 when the monks of St. Werburgh were asked to "to have care of ye olde yew". Some of the Shropshire Trees suggest they are far older than the one at Eastham.

The great yew tree at Claverley, over 8 metres (29 feet) girth, is one of the largest and oldest in the county. It stands to the east end of the church and is almost completely hollow. The churchyard in which it stands is the focal point for this charming village. This site bears all the signs that it is pre-Christian. It is on a mound, it has an embankment around it and it stands above a brook. What

Church Preen Yew – Shropshire's most celebrated yew.

is more conclusive is the account of the restoration work that was carried out on the church in 1902 when the whole of the Nave and Chancel were opened up and the floor lowered to its original level. Here is an extract from the *History of Claverley* by W. H. Dawkes.

"Whilst the work was in progress it became obvious that the old custom of inter-rural burial had been extensively practised in Claverley.

The floor of the Nave was lowered approximately three feet and many human remains were reverently removed and buried in the churchyard.

A platform was laid above, extending under the whole of the Nave from the Chancel steps to within six feet of the west wall. It had an average depth of three feet, but its west end was seven feet deep and in the form of a buttress. This platform was built of rough, unhewn stone, set in concrete.

The ground had been excavated for it and authorities were convinced that it was of Roman origin. Later, as the work proceeded, further interesting discoveries were made. At the north eastern end of the platform near the place where the pulpit now stands, human remains were discovered.

The bones were those of a man, a child and a small animal. The bodies were lying north to south, not east to west and so the burial was obviously pagan. With the bodies a small urn was buried and this might easily have been Saxon. The deciding factor in thinking the burial to be Roman was the fact that the small animal had been buried with the child as well as the urn.

The interment being pagan would indicate the time of burial to be prior to the Declaration of Christianity by Constantine in the 4th century and, therefore, of Romano-British date.

Antiquaries and authorities generally are of the opinion that the platform was the site of a small building at the point where the Roman roads converged. Whether the building was pagan or Christian we cannot say, but we do know that Christian churches existed in Britain as early as the 2nd century."

There seems well recorded proof that this churchyard had been in use for a considerable time before the Norman church was built. The yew tree certainly looks as if it pre-dates the present church by a very considerable margin. Recent research by Alan Meredith may indicate that the age of any yew tree of this girth and character could be in the region of 1,500 years.

Surrounding Ashford Carbonel church are five very large yews, three female (bearing fruit) and two male trees. It is unusual to find five large yews on one site. As mentioned a 19th century quote says that local villagers state that the trees are over 1,500 years old. But how long could they have been saying that?

A similar churchyard is found at Acton Scott where five ancient trees are located (2 male and 3 female). One tree displays an unusual characteristic; that of an 'internal stem' growing within the hollow trunk — a clear case of self-regeneration.

The yew tree at Church Preen is one of the most celebrated and most well known yews in Britain. It is certainly the most recorded yew in Shropshire. In the *History of Church Preen* by Arthur Sparrow are many details about the tree's size over the last few centuries. The earliest measurement was taken in 1780 and the circumference then was 32 feet 2 inches around the base (at 4ft from the ground it measured 19 feet). In 1833 it was 22 feet (at 4 feet) and in 1897 it was 22 feet 4 inches. Measuring in June 1983, again at 4 feet from the ground, the tree was 6.9

metres (22 feet 8 inches); slightly larger than it measured in 1897. It is difficult to draw firm conclusions from these measurements, but it is plain to see the tree is only showing a minimal increase in girth size.

An iron band placed round the tree over a century ago still exists. This band may be detrimental to the tree's health in the future. The Frenchman, de Candolle, estimated the tree to be about 1,400 years old in 1831 and Dr. John Lowe estimated it to be 750 to 1,000 years old in 1897. The tree is very hollow and curiously 21 people were reputed to have stood within it in 1897. It is a very tall tree for a yew and has a majestic appearance with a good clean bole. This tree is without doubt older than the extremely narrow and interesting chapel close by. Another yew close to the bathing pool in the private garden measured 19 feet 3 inches (at 4 feet) in 1897; it is now just over 6 metres (20 feet). The travel writer, Fletcher Moss, wrote in 1890 "the beautiful old female yew tree laced with myriads of fruit on which innumerable birds were feasting"; with scrupulous attention to detail he reported that he leant his bicycle against the tree. The local poet, Beatrice Pinches (aged 91), wrote the following in 1983:

"Oh Ancient tree how many dawns
Have you seen flaring up the sky
How many stilly noons and eves
When sunshine loved your outstretched arms
And dappled the hard earth about your roots.

How many summer moons have waxed and waned
Winters, when cold winds buffeted your boughs
And birds sought shelter from the blast
Springs when cuckoos called o'er Wenlock Edge
And May trees stood in drifts of white.

So much has passed beneath your shade,
The happy bride with light-some step
The mourner bowed with measured tread,
Pacing towards an open grave.
Those homeless Wenlock monks who sought
Sanctuary in this quiet place

And built, with patience stone by stone
Their home and church that stand today
I seem to hear their chanting
In fancy when the evening comes,
And the padding of their sandalled feet
As to their humble tasks they go.

How changeless in a changing world
In this green and quiet glade,
Where one can almost feel that time
Itself stands still and pausing,
breathless, listens."

The tree in Clun churchyard is possibly the oldest in the county. It measures over 10.5 metres (34 feet) around the remaining pieces of the base. It is very decayed and an excavation was carried out around the tree in May 1946 by Tom Beardsley of Clun. Noting that the present tree was growing from an older shell and that the tree appeared as if growing on a mound (quite common with ancient yews) he decided to excavate around the base in an attempt to locate the 'original' trunk. This he did and measured it at 10.3 metres (33 feet 9 inches) girth. Tom Beardsley's theory was that the mound had been caused by grave excavation material being thrown under the tree over the centuries causing the original base to be hidden. He seems to have been proven right. Mr. Beardsley has also received information from the Science Museum to the effect that a large group of yews were felled on an island in the Lake District during the Second World War and that most of the trees were solid. A tree of 6.7 metres (22 feet) girth showed 900 annual rings. On these calculations the original Clun yew would be well over 2,000 years old. The Clun tree though is not solid and it would have probably taken hundreds of years to decay before it started to regrow, so how old can it be? The yew is mentioned in the book *All around the Wrekin* (1860) as "a patriachal yew which looks as old if not older than the church itself".

There is much historical evidence from the Clun Valley to support the view that quite a large community existed in that area for thousands of years before Christ and it is entirely feasible that the Clun churchyard was used as a holy site back into the Celtic period and before.

At Dudleston in the north of Shropshire a Saxon cross stands next to the Norman church and several old yews stand on the perimeter of the churchyard. The oldest of these trees is very hollow and has an iron band around its trunk. During restoration work on the church in the 19th century the church bell was hung in the tree until work to the bell tower was completed. There is also a well in this churchyard, again suggesting an old site.

The murder of the patron of Easthope Church in 1333 has given the churchyard the reputation of being haunted. In it is also buried the remains of two monks from the nearby hall who killed each other in a drunken fight. The Norman church was burnt down earlier this century and the one now standing is

Church Preen Yew,
showing the iron band.

Loughton Yew, showing the contorted trunk of this massive tree.

a modern replacement. The circular nature of this site certainly suggests that it is of ancient origin. An ancient yew, girth 7 metres (23 feet) with over a quarter of the trunk now gone, stands on the site.

A most interesting yew tree is to be found in the churchyard at Hope Bagot, south Shropshire. Younger yews border the lane descending to the church. The oldest tree, over 7 metres (23 feet) in girth and with huge branches spreading over the lane, is a majestic specimen. The other major item of interest is the holy well in the bank directly below the tree. A spring is also located across the road. It seems hard not to connect what is obviously an ancient tree with the well and the old churchyard. Younger yews also lined an old track which led from the churchyard up the bank towards Clee Hill. These have unfortunately been felled.

A Roman altar that was found buried in Uppington churchyard when alterations were made early this century, now stands beside one of the county's oldest trees. In the 1880s the tree measured 8.7 metres (26 feet 6 inches) girth and now measures 8.8 metres (29 feet) — it is completely hollow. Allowing two centuries of initial 'rapid' growth at the slower rate of growth recorded during the last 100 years the tree would be just over 1,000 years old. A watercolour painting by Rev. Williams in the 1790s shows two large yews at Uppington. The tree shown to the west of the church has now gone, probably removed during restoration work. This has been known to happen at other churchyards and is still unfortunately happening today.

In the remote village of Loughton, below the Brown Clee Hill, a small stone chapel stands upon a classic pre-Christian site. It contains, as with Clun, what appears to be one of the oldest living things in Shropshire. The massive contorted bole of the female yew over 9 metres (30 feet measured at 2ft from ground) is hollow and is used as a shelter by the sheep who keep the grass of the

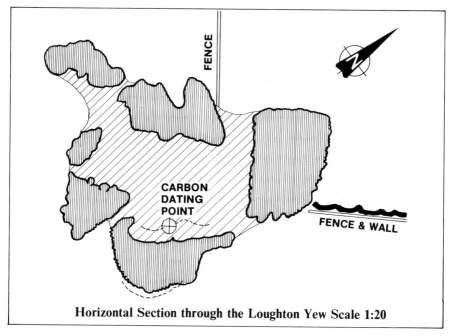

Horizontal Section through the Loughton Yew Scale 1:20

churchyard closely cropped. In 1986 the Shropshire branch of the CPRE took a sample of wood from the tree and this was carbon dated at Cambridge University. The sample was taken from inside the hollow trunk and was determined to be 550 years old (plus or minus 50 years), thus making the date of the sample 1435 AD.

It is estimated that the tree would have taken in excess of 400 years to grow to the sampling point. So an age around 1,000 years for the tree is, indicated.

The earliest record of a chapel here is 1291. What structure, if any, preceded this is not known. What seems quite certain is that the yew tree did. The Yew at Loughton was the first in the world to receive the carbon dating method.

Ruyton-XI-Towns has a female yew that used to have the main stem propped up; that has now fallen but younger growth maintains the tree's existence. The wall erected before 1790 around the Norbury male yew is still there but the massive tree, the largest but not necessarily the oldest yew in Shropshire, is beginning to grow into the wall. Again this churchyard is of ancient origin.

Yew trees in the countryside

Yew trees occur less frequently in the open countryside outside of churchyards. As a general rule, they are usually far younger than the churchyard yews.

There is one exceptional case which really falls into the 'churchyard' category. Although the yews are in fact outside the churchyard. This enigma is the **twin yews of Middleton Scriven.** These are the strangest and most unusual yews in the county because of their problematic location.

These massive yews, female 8.83 metres (29 feet), male 8.53 metres (28 feet), are to be found standing alone in a field facing across a lane to the church. There is an immediate sense of displacement. They are quite plainly 'churchyard yews' but on the wrong side of the road.

The present church is a small handsome building from the Victorian period . . . It is known from the Rev. Williams' accurate watercolour paintings of 1790 that a Norman Chapel preceded the present church on the same site. This was probably of 12th century vintage.

There, so far, the enigma ends . . . almost. The thought occurs that if a church occupied this site prior to the Norman church it would, of course, have been Saxon. If late Saxon it would have been stone; if early Saxon it would have been constructed of wood.

There is an unwritten village story concerning a wooden church which was burnt down. The story insists that it stood by the twin yews.

Marker yews
Throughout the county can be found remnant lines of yew trees that mark old routes and boundaries across the countryside. These 'marker' trees are often to be found leading towards parish churches and chapels.

There are also yews found growing alone in fields. Either these trees have been

Twin Yews, Middleton Scriven. Aerial photograph 1985 showing location of yews in field opposite the present church. Was the churchyard moved in the medieval period?

left because of the superstition that to fell a yew brings misfortune, or because the trees formed part of a 'marking system now lost or destroyed.

The dark foliage of the yew is easy to pick out in the landscape. In the Summer the crown is darker than all other trees and in the Winter the evergreen appearance is easily distinguished from long distances. Even today people occasionally use these trees as 'guiding points' or landmarks on walks. In times when all country folk attended Sunday church services, many coming on foot, the yews must have been valuable 'signposts'.

We must not, though, run away with the idea that all yews in the countryside are marking mysterious trails. The yew is indigenous to certain localities in the county and can be common in these areas particularly in woodlands where it can grow under the densest shade. Some examples of localities where the yew grows wild are around Wenlock Edge on the limestone, on the Wrekin/Ercall ridge, the side of Acton Burnell hill and the Ironbridge Gorge woodlands.

The practice, from Elizabethan days until the last century, to plant the yew near dwellings, principally to provide shelter, is another factor to be considered. Care then is required in identifying genuine 'marker' trees. Below is a list of remnant lines of yews already identified.

Acton Burnell
There are many yew trees on Acton Burnell hill. One tree has a girth of over 7 metres (23 feet) and several others are over 6 metres (20 feet). Some of the biggest yews follow closely the parish boundary that cuts along the ridge of the hill. An area called 'Yew Tree Piece' contains between twenty and thirty big healthy trees that are younger than the others. The yew seeds readily over this land.

Acton Round
Yews border the medieval track that once lead from Shirlett Forest down the hill towards Acton Round church.

Benthall
There are several large yews on the woodland edge that may well have been boundary markers. Also several trees can be found in neighbouring fields close to the place called 'The Vineyards'. Yews in hedgerows mark the parish boundary of Benthall and Barrow.

Easthope
Yews can be found in fields along bridleways, in hedgerows, in woodland and by cottages all around this area. Some of these trees, in fields, have been left undisturbed for centuries despite having the reputation of being highly poisonous to livestock. The churchyard at Easthope is the focal point for many of these trees.

Hine Heath

There are several hedgerow yews bordering the Hodnet-Preston Brockhurst road below the Bury Walls camp.

Hope Bagot

There are several yews on the boundary of the lane leading down the hill towards Hope Bagot churchyard. A line of yews following a footpath and track that leads to the church was recently felled.

Longden

The lane between Plealey and Longden contains yews in bordering hedgerows. There are also yews in nearby field hedgerows.

Long Mynd

Above Myndtown several very old yews are to be found by tracks on the side of the Long Mynd. An area named 'Yew Tree Batch' can be found close to Yapsul Spring not far from the Glider Club although there are no yews growing there now.

Loughton

Leading down the lanes and hedgerows towards the huge old Loughton churchyard yew can be found somewhat younger yews. One has a girth exceeding 5 metres (16 feet 3 inches).

Middlehope

Yews marking footpaths lead up from Middlehope towards Wenlock Edge. They eventually lead on to paths in the Munslow area.

Munslow

A remnant avenue of yews leads down to Munslow church along the old bridleway called 'Munslow Deans', sometimes referred to as 'The Pilgrims Way', the supposed route of the pilgrims, who in the Middle Ages came from Wenlock Abbey to Ludlow and then on to Hereford Cathedral. A 'Pilgrims Cottage' located on the path gives added credence, to the supposed route. Also it is known that the hill called the 'Speller', was once used as a gathering place in the Middle Ages for the local 'moot' or court. The name 'Speller' is derived from the Saxon word 'Spel' meaning speech. The Speller is located next to the bridleway. Further investigation into this area could prove rewarding.

Marker Yew, Easthope – remnant lines of yews can be found in various parts of the county.

Nedge Hill, Telford
A prominent yew on the top of Nedge Hill can be seen from miles around and could well have been planted as a landmark.

Penkridge Hall, Leebotwood
The hall is located below the Lawley Hill. In medieval times it was the Shropshire headquarters of the Knights Templar. In front of the hall are two yews with a known planting date of 1509. One tree has a girth of 2.5 metres (8 feet 3 inches) and is approximately 40 feet tall. The other tree is shorter but has a girth of 3 metres (10 feet 2 inches). It is rare to find such an early recorded planting date.

Richards Castle
Old yews can be found in the hedgerow bordering the lane connecting Richards Castle and Ashford Carbonel.

Norbury Yew – one of the Shropshire giants. The tree is now growing into the wall built around its base pre-1800.

Sidbury Yew – an old yew in an old churchyard. Unfortunately the hollow trunks of these trees are often the place to store unwanted churchyard materials. See 'Future of Churchyard Yew' in Appendices.

Sidbury

The footpaths converging onto Sidbury Church are marked by old yews.

Stottesdon

The village and church at Stottesdon stand on a hill and yews can be found in the hedgerows that lead up towards the village.

None of the countryside yews examined achieve the great age of the oldest of the churchyard yews with the exception of the twin yews of Middleton Scriven. The huge trees on Acton Burnell hill come closest in age and girth size, and elsewhere a few 20 feet girth trees can be found, but they are a rarity. The 'marker' yews have been planted far later than the ancient churchyard yews. They range in girth from about 2 metres (6 feet 6 inches) to about 5 metres (16 feet 3 inches), 3.5/4.0 metres (11 feet 3 inches/13 feet) being the more usual size found.

Taking the Penkridge Hall recorded planting date and comparing sizes it appears that some of the marker trees could be as old as six hundred years, but it seems more likely that they date from the 16th and 17th centuries, whilst some of the smaller trees may be 18th century plantings. The known variation in growth rates of individual yew trees must be taken into account and means that age assessment is very approximate, for example the 1777 planting of the West Felton Yew, which had a girth in 1984 of 3.65 metres (12 feet) shows some yews grow far faster than others in the first two hundred years or so.

It must be emphasised that the above list is not comprehensive for the whole of the county, more research is required into the location of the 'marker' yews and into the origin of their planting. It is known that the practice of planting landmark yews occurs in several other parts of the country, e.g. Herefordshire, Oxfordshire, South Downs. The most famous being the trees flanking the Pilgrims Way between Winchester and Canterbury.

The Oaks

"The Monarch Oak, the patriarch of trees
shoots rising up and spreads by low degrees
Three centuries he grows and three he stays
Supreme in state, and in three more decays."

Dryden

After the churchyard yews come the pollard oaks. It is possible for an oak to live a thousand years.

The Gospel Oak at Polstead, Suffolk must have been about that age when it finally collapsed early this century. The Polstead tree had been a boundary oak at which the annual celebration of 'beating the bounds' (walking the parish boundary) had been practised for many centuries. In some parishes the custom is still carried out today. Under the branches of a 'gospel oak' passages of the scriptures are recited in order to protect the parish against evil spirits. This old custom was inaugurated by Avitus, Bishop of Vienna, in 800 AD.

Examples of the existence of boundary oaks are preserved in some Shropshire place names. The area called 'Meer' Oak, near Church Preen is located on the parish boundary between Ruckley and Langley. 'Meer' is a Saxon word meaning boundary. Another 'Meer Oak' can be found near Chapel Lawn. The Ale Oak near Mainstone in South West Shropshire derives its name not from beer but from a corruption of "hale", another Saxon 'boundary' word. There are several places named Round Oak which again are likely places where boundary oaks once stood.

As with the yews it can be very illuminating to look at the area in which great oaks stand. It is not sufficient simply to look at the trees alone. The pattern of land, topography and history of the landscape surrounding the tree can give many clues as to why the tree is there and why it has survived.

The Shropshire Oaks

One of Shropshire's great oaks, the **Acton Round Oak** located by the side of a track that follows the ridge between Acton Round and Monkhall, is a case in point. The tree is one of the country's biggest sessile oaks with a girth of over 8.83 metres (29 feet). It is an old 'pollard' tree, the branches having been regularly cut back. It is very hollow but grows a perfectly healthy crown of leaves each Spring. Why has it survived? More than likely it is a survivor from remnants of the original Shirlett Forest that once covered the hillsides around Acton Round. The word 'Shirlett' is derived from "share of the shire" meaning that the woodland was once a major part of the original Norman "Shropshire" Royal Forest. Shirlett Forest was included in the great forestry perambulation of 1300 and individual trees are mentioned in the document as boundary markers. "Yapenacres Merwey up to Ravenshok (Ravens Oak) and Coalheath to

Fendehok (Fiends Oak)". Even earlier, in 1256, records exist that include reference to a land dispute between John Fitzalan of Acton and the Prior of Wenlock. Taken from *Antiquities of Shropshire Vol. 4* is the following account:-

> "The Assize roll of January 1256 reports of a Perambulation made by precept of the King, between land of John Fitzalan in Acton and the land of the Prior of Wenlock in Burgton and Calweton (Calloughton). Part of the Wood of Spoonhull was in question. The boundary determined mentioned an oak tree "Ronsak" which stood upon the King's highway between Weston and Wenlock, also another large *(grosum)* oak tree which stood upon Corve toward the West".

The position described fits well with the location of the oak now standing by the track. If 'Ronsak' is the Acton Round Oak then it is well over eight hundred years old.

Acton Round Oak. The old pollard tree still grows beside the track that crosses the ridge where Shirlett Forest once grew.

Acton Round Oak, showing the interesting hollow trunk.

Early in the Middle Ages Wenlock Priory set up four woodland hamlets in the forest. The places still exist in name: Monkhall, Harpers Monkhall, Masons Monkhall and Woodhouse Field. A derelict woodland township can also be traced at Spoonhill Wood close to the Acton Round Oak. The track which winds its way past the Oak was once an important route through the woodland. It is now merely a farm track and footpath. To have escaped the woodland clearance it must have had some particular importance and it seems reasonable to suggest it may have been retained to mark the boundary of some parcel of land. Here is a good example of how examining the history of the area in which a tree stands can give valuable information about the tree itself.

The term 'wood pasture', mentioned in the opening chapter often has very close connections with the great oaks. This system of management allowed livestock to graze and forage below the 'pollard' trees, the lower branches would be browsed and acorns foraged when available.

The grazing of cattle and deer on the land however always prevented new growth as the ground was trampled hard and grass vegetation took over the herb layer. Thus typical wood pasture was grass beneath trees which developed a 'browsing line' beneath their crowns. Oaks in wood pasture were usually spaced at about twelve to the acre and were regularly pollarded; which had the effect of increasing the longevity of the tree. The demands from the normally ever increasing crown were reduced and the likelihood of boughs breaking from wind damage disappeared. Pollard management was carried out throughout the medieval period and into the Middle Ages on a major scale. It occurred on the common land of the manor, 'waste' areas and in the enclosed parks, where red deer and cattle were the domestic livestock.

The appearance of stag-headed oaks in the present-day countryside is probably an indication that the tree is naturally limiting its 'fuel network', a sort of 'self-pollarding' system. All the giant oaks of Shropshire have been pollarded in the past.

When oaks become old they are host to an incredibly rich 'natural history' of their own. They become mini nature reserves. Birds, invertebrates, and lichens especially thrive, and some of the lichens have been found to contain antibiotics that repel damaging wood decaying fungi.

One of the most interesting and complete examples of an early deer park is Melbury Park in Dorset. Here some ancient pollards can still be found. The trees have quaint names, one called 'Billy Wilkins' has a girth just short of 12 metres (39 feet 5 inches). It is one of Britain's oldest and biggest oaks. Very similar to Billy Wilkins in appearance and stature is the **Lydham Manor Oak,** near Bishop's Castle, this huge and impressive oak is one of the country's largest girthed trees. It is certainly the county's largest recorded oak by some 1 metre and in Britain only the Bowthorpe Oak at Whitham-on-the-Hill in Lincolnshire is larger. The Lydham tree has a hugely burred trunk, covered in lichens and mosses. Other vegetation grows on it, including hollies and elder.

The practice of pollarding having ceased, it is probable that the tree experienced rapid increase in girth as a result. In 1946 the tree measured 10.36 metres (34 feet), in 1984 it was a little under 12 metres (39 feet). A remarkable increase of 1.60 metres (5 feet) in 30 years. Continuing at its present rate of growth, the Lydham Manor Oak has the chance of becoming the largest girthed oak in Britain in 10 or more years time. Maybe for its own good though it should again be pollarded.

Billy Wilkins is estimated to be between six and eight hundred years old. The Lydham Manor Oak can be counted also in those terms.

The old name for the Lydham estate was Oakley Park and it seems more than likely that the big oak was once part of a medieval enclosed park. Growing as it does though on the brow of a hill it may also have had some greater significance which has been lost over the centuries.

All tree growth at Lydham is exceptional. Next to the driveway leading up to the Manor House is another very impressive oak of 9 metres (30 feet) girth. This tree has a clean smooth trunk apart from a split which appears to be caused by excessive branch weight, due to the neglect of traditional management practices. A cable has been inserted in the main branches in an effort to keep the crown together.

Lydham Manor has also a very large sessile oak, two huge walnuts and the county record for a fern leaved beech.

At Oakly Park, Bromfield, near Ludlow, the **Druid Oaks** have now sadly almost all gone. These trees must also have been part of an earlier enclosed deer park similar to Melbury Park and Lydham. Documentary evidence exists to show that this area has been managed as a park for many centuries.

Standing at Crowleasowes Farm, near Bitterley on the fringe of the original Clee Forest is the **Crowleasowes Oak,** an impressive hulk of a tree that is second only in size of trunk to the big oak at Lydham Manor. In fact for some considerable time it was the county's largest tree with a girth of over 11 metres (36 feet).

Lydham Manor Oak, one of Shropshire's greatest trees.

Inevitably this oak is a hollow pollarded tree but unlike some great oaks has been regularly cropped of its branches until fairly recently. The new growth from the old trunk is healthy and green and there seems no reason why the tree will not continue to live for many centuries yet. Attached to its trunk are bits of ironwork put there by the Victorians to help to keep it together. Its huge hollow centre must have been used as a delightful play 'cave' for countless children over the years.

There are two references from the Victorian period that describe the tree. Oliver Baker in *Ludlow Town and Neighbourhood* 1889 talks of "an oak of gigantic girth". H. Thornhill-Timmins writing in *Nooks and Corners of Shropshire* 1889 describes on the approach to Crowleasowes Farmhouse an oak with a gigantic girth but hollow within, flings its vast limbs athwart the greensward before the entrance way".

The Crowleasowes Oak seems a likely survivor from the old Clee Forest. The Forest of Clee extended over a relatively small area of 24,000 acres and ceased being a Royal Forest as early as 1155. It was continued as a privately managed estate by the Clifford family from Corfham Castle after that date. The forest which was mainly open land, covered the Brown Clee Hill and surrounding areas. By the Middle Ages most of the woodland timber had been felled, apart from some coppices that were still attached to the manors. The farmhouse at Crowleasowes is a superb Jacobean period building in front of which stands a restored cider press.

Growing directly above a spring close to Holt Farm near the village of Plaish is another of Shropshire's giant pollard oaks. The massive **Holt Preen Oak** is of

Holt Preen Oak, the wall below it encloses the underground spring.

Forest Oak, Quatford. The legend goes back to the 11th century.

obvious great age and stature. Measured in 1983 it had a girth of 8.8 (28 feet 6 inches) metres at 1.2 metres (3 feet 9 inches).

The water issuing from beneath its cavernous roots is pure and very cold. Until 1984 this spring supplied the village of Plaish with drinking water. A large stone trough has been built very close to the tree and around it there is a stone wall with a wooden gate. The wall is believed to have been built at the same time as the farmhouse, which is of 16th century date.

From the trough, the spring water is piped to two large well constructed underground stone chambers hidden beneath the field, a short distance from the tree. One chamber houses a three piston pumping engine, the other a 15 foot diameter 'overshot' water wheel. This wheel was driven by piped water diverted from the nearby stream.

The wheel and pumping engine, now unused and in disrepair, were replaced by an electric pump housed in a small brick building in the field close by, after the Second World War.

The village of Plaish was only put onto mains water supply in 1984. The spring beneath the oak must come from deep underground for even in the hottest Summer it never dries up nor does its temperature rise. The farmer tells of a man being unable to collect a fallen object from the trough during one of the hottest Summer days of 1976 because the water was too cold.

The combination of oak tree and spring used to be of great significance and legends go back at least as far as the biblical story of Aaron's Rod. This particular tree though is of fairly recent antiquity and is probably between 400 and 600 years old. What can be said is that in the days when the original forest clearances were made in this locality the strength of folklore memory would have been much stronger than it is now and the existence of an oak tree and spring would have been thought worthy of preservation.

The tree is now stag-headed and declining but there is still some good young growth to be seen.

Another heavily burred old pollard oak, growing close to water, and which ranks with the county's largest and oldest is the **Powis Oak.** This classically shaped ancient oak, stands near a stream and wood close to Underhill Hall. The Hall, as the name implies, sits romantically on the gentle northerly slopes of the Long Mynd between Picklescott and Pulverbatch.

The Powis Oak takes its name from the Powis family who used to live at Underhill Hall and who achieved distinction in various walks of life. The area around Underhill contains other interesting features including a plaque marking

Frodesley Oak, last survivor of many old trees near the Lodge.

the old estate boundary and some ancient earthworks near Wilderley Hill.

At Frodesley Lodge, 200 metres (217 yards) up the side of Lodge Hill close to Hoar Edge and the Causeway can be found the Frodesley Oak.

At the turn of the century the travel writer Fletcher Moss visited Frodesley Lodge on his bicycle looking for material for his publication *Pilgrimages in Cheshire and Shropshire*. He found the Lodge commanding an impressive view over North Shropshire and the westerly hill regions and described some "decrepit old oaks that stood in a state of decay below the Lodge". At the Lodge he met a woman who insisted that Fletcher was her long lost son. Even after assuring her that he was not she continued to believe that he was and the memory of the incident lived with Moss for many years.

One of the "decrepit" oaks described by Moss still stands and hangs determinedly on to life with a few fresh leaves appearing each year. The girth of

Frodesley Lodge. A wood print from Fletcher Moss's 'Pilgrimages in Cheshire and Shropshire' at the turn of the century depicted the Lodge and gnarled old oaks.

FRODESLEY LODGE

HIGH up, on an outlying spur at the end of the steep hill known as Hoar Edge, about ten miles south of Shrewsbury, there is a curious house or castle standing forth prominently on a precipitous

FRODESLEY LODGE

Dryton Oak, Eaton Constantine. A great tree growing close to where the Watch Oak stood.

the Frodesley Oak was 7.77 metres (25 feet 6 inches) in 1946 and is only slightly more now because the rate of growth will have virtually been zero for many decades.

Fletcher Moss described the scene as he saw it in the early 1900s as a hillside scattered with several old oaks. An evocative drawing contained in his book shows the house standing on a steep sided hill in front of which are two old pollard oaks. We can therefore be reasonably certain that the surviving tree was once part of the 'wood pasture' which was incorporated into the enclosed part of

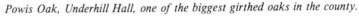

Powis Oak, Underhill Hall, one of the biggest girthed oaks in the county.

The Nash Oak

Frodesley. The park boundary (Park Pale) can apparently still be traced in field divisions, and a wall built in 1609 near Park Farm is still standing. The deer park that once existed has long since gone, but the old oak is without doubt a relic of the original estate management system. According to Rowley the house at Frodesley was a 17th century hunting lodge.

In the extreme south of the county, close to the junction between the Burford/Coreley road and Whatmore/Nash lane, stands an old pollard oak in an advanced stage of decay. The tree is called the **Nash Oak** and had a girth of 8.8 metres (29 feet) in 1983. It grows on the field edge opposite a large farmhouse. In 1984 the dead limbs were cut back in an attempt to revive the tree. It seems that the tree's decline may have been hastened by a lightning strike.

Trees were often used as landmarks for travellers as it was not until 1720 that milestones were put by roadsides. The Mile Oak has long since gone from the outskirts of Oswestry but the name remains. In fact the name Oswestry is supposedly derived from 'Oswald's Tree'. Mile Oaks survive in other regions and even Turnpike Oaks. These large hollow trees used as toll collection shelters, existed into the early part of this century.

The Mawley Oak situated near the junction of the B4202 and the A4117 Bewdley to Cleobury Mortimer road is another example of a landmark tree. It marked the meeting of two woodland tracks on the outskirts of the Wyre Forest in the Middle Ages.

Norman Hickin states in his book *The Natural History of an English Forest* that he inspected and measured the tree in October 1968. The girth was then 7.16

metres (23 feet 6 inches) giving a diameter of 2.28 metres (7.5 feet). There was, he calculated, 1417 square yards of ground covered by foliage; a quarter of an acre. It had about 30 main branches, one of which was home for a colony of honey bees. He estimated the height of the tree as 26 metres (86 feet). The bark was heavily 'fissured' and a wren's nest was found in a crevice.

A major limb broke out of the tree in the 1970s and a large ineffectively treated wound can now be observed. Inevitably it would seem the tree was once a pollard oak, but because the branches have been allowed to grow freely into the ample space around the tree, the resultant massive growth has caused limb breakage — excessive weight having over-stressed the junction of the main branch with the bole.

The Mawley Oak takes its name from nearby Mawley Hall. It has not got a particularly large trunk but its huge spreading crown and location make it one of the most majestic sights of the Wyre Forest area.

The Wyre Forest is itself a fascinating place and other interesting trees can be found there, including the Goodmoor Oak, a huge coppiced tree called the Seckley Beech and the celebrated Witty Pear. The forest is a National Nature Reserve and at the Visitor Centre information on the history of the forest and its management is imaginatively displayed. The major part of the forest is in Worcestershire but the site of the now vanished Button Oak, once a much loved tree, is in Shropshire. Nearby is a public house called 'The Button Oak'.

One of Shropshire's largest forests in the medieval period was the Long Forest which covered most of the land between Meole Brace and Craven Arms and stretched from Cressage in the east to Wentnor and Longden in the west. The forest was finally enclosed in 1527 and by 1616 it was practically cleared.

One tree that may well be a survivor from the edge of the Long Forest is the **Lady Oak** of Cressage. This tree is now no more than a huge hulk of wood supported by a younger oak that has either grown from an acorn dropped by the mother tree, or has been planted deliberately as a replacement for the old Lady Oak. In its heyday the Lady Oak will have been a well-known landmark to all travellers on the Bridgnorth to Shrewsbury road.

The sad but impressive remains of the old tree now stand rather strangely in an open field (Near Lady Oak Leasow) between the disused Severn Valley Railway line and the A458. The original winding road, the alignment of which was altered when the railway was built in 1861, passed right beside the tree and then on to Cound Lodge, skirting it on the River Severn side, not as today. The Baugh map of 1808 shows the original road. During the drought of 1976 the position of the old road could be seen crossing the fields past the tree. Not far away is the site of the now demolished Saxon Church of St. Samson, its original position now marked by a cross.

Amongst the earlier written records of the tree is an account of a fire lit inside the hollow trunk early in the 19th century. A copy of this account can be found in Cound church, it reads:

"The Lady Oak in this neighbourhood is nearly demolished.

Fire carelessly made too near the tree communicated with the hollow and decayed parts causing its destruction on 25th June 1814. Fortunately a sketch was made of the venerable tree and dimensions were taken which are maybe worth preserving."

Lady Oak, Cressage – the old relic leans on the younger offspring.

*Lady Oak
of Cressage.*

They are as follows:-

    Girth Bottom 41 feet 7 inches (12.67 metres)
    Girth Middle 24 feet 2 inches (7.36 metres)
    Girth under Boughs 26 feet 5 inches (8.05m)

One theory suggests that gypsies who regularly camped under the shelter of the tree may have accidentally left a fire burning when they moved on.

The Victorian antiquarians took a deep interest in the Lady Oak and in 1876 when the Severn Valley Railway was in regular use a rail traveller wrote "The Cressage Oak, so well known to Salopians standing within view of the railway line from Shrewsbury to Bridgnorth, well exhibits a younger tree growing within the hollow of the parent bole, taller already than its progenitor and will ultimately succeed to the title and occupation of its decrepit sire". About the same time an Edward Lees measured the tree and found it to be 8.53 metres (28 feet) near the base. In 1877 a long article appeared in the *Gardeners' Chronicle* by

H. Eversheds. He mentioned the fire damage and noted that the tree had fifteen living branches 15 feet to 20 feet long.

In 1915 the tree was fenced off, it then had about two thirds of its trunk left, which was propped up by four stays and several wooden props.

It also had an iron clamp around its trunk. Inside the shell were many carved initials. By 1950 the old branches were still bearing acorns. The tree finally died

An early postcard shows the young oak growing through the hollow trunk of the ancient Lady Oak.

CRESSAGE OAK, SHROPSHIRE.   WILDING. 1588

in the severe frosts of January 1982. The decline in the tree's health was probably accelerated by the removal of the protective fence which allowed deep ploughing and fertiliser applications right below the tree's crown, a fact which is borne out by the dieback present in the younger oak. Nevertheless for a tree which was termed 'nearly demolished' in 1814 it did well to hang on to life for another 170 years after the fire.

The Victorians suggested the tree could in fact have been the actual oak from which Cressage took its name. The Saxon name for Cressage was Christache meaning Christ's Oak. It was also suggested that St. Augustine preached below the tree around 584 AD. It seems to be stretching credibility beyond the bounds of reason to give the Lady Oak that sort of age.

It is more likely that the name Christ's Oak (Christache) is connected with the Welsh St. Samson who travelled widely and who is known to have set up a church next to a great river in this region in the 6th century.

The Lady Oak is probably no more than eight hundred years old and no less than six hundred. A clue to her age can be found in the name. It was often the practice in the 13th and 14th centuries to bestow religious names on well known objects. The honouring of a tree with the Virgin Mother's name could be an explanation. H. G. D. Foxall's book *Shropshire Field Names* mentions a "Lady Meadow" and "Ladywell" indicating dedication to the Virgin Mary for the maintenance of a shrine or chapel. The tree may have been so dedicated.

Another possible explanation of the name is that it is a corruption of "Law Day". These days, particularly in Scotland, were held for the Local Assizes, similar to the 'moots'. The tree could have been the location for the local court.

In Brampton Bryan in Herefordshire there once stood a 'Laugh Lady Oak' which again may have been a corruption of "Law Day". Strangely though the name Lady Oak is not common in other counties.

At Plox Green, near Minsterley there stood until the 1950s another Lady Oak. It grew close to the old Shrewsbury to Bishop's Castle road. The hollow tree was felled because it was deemed to be dangerous. It was by all accounts, and having seen the stump, a huge tree with branches spreading right across the road. It is believed to have been used in the construction of Worthen church in the 13th century. The locality is still known as Lady Oak and Lady Oak Villa stands closeby.

Another story connects the Lady Oak of Cressage with the author, satirist and cleric, Jonathon Swift (1667-1745), who wrote *Gulliver's Travels*. Travelling through Cressage, Swift sheltered under the Lady Oak during a summer thunderstorm. Also sheltering were a young couple both soaking wet. A conversation started naturally about the weather but soon the couple nervously admitted to Dean Swift that they were eloping and were looking for a clergyman to marry them. Jonathon Swift said he was such a man and married them there and then under the tree.

It is known that Swift visited Shrewsbury, so the story may well be true, and he did write a poem about the incident.

> *"Under an oak in stormy weather*
> *I joined this rogue and whore together*
> *Let none but the God who makes the thunder,*
> *E'er put this whore and rogue asunder."*

A nice story and who will argue with its authenticity!

Another category of old oaks, slightly divorced from the previous ones mentioned is concerned with the trees that have distinct historical associations.

These stories and legends have built up over time so as to now be as much a part of the tree as the wood itself. Some of the stories are true. Some rather dubious in their authenticity but all are worth relating.

In other countries similar legends are often inextricably bound up with trees. The species concerned though is not always oak. For example in Germany old large-leaved lime trees often have stories associated with them. People still display great affection for their old giants that stand in town squares or at some important crossroads.

In Britain, and particularly England, the trees with stories are, more often than not, old oak trees. For example the Major Oak, Sherwood Forest, Nottinghamshire has historical associations with Robin Hood. Each county has its sprinkling of legendary oaks with many of the legends having gained fresh impetus during the Victorian era.

Age determination of these relic oaks is difficult as with all old unrecorded trees but is somewhat easier than trying to judge the age of ancient yews.

Although oak trees grow less erratically than yews, old ones often are hollow and with the rotting of the heartwood goes the possibility of counting the annual rings.

Tracking down information on vanished oaks can usefully start with a glance over the Ordnance Survey map. There are many name references to oaks which no longer exist. A good example of a locality named after a lost tree probably of fairly recent demise is 'Shade Oak' which describes simply and poetically a place near Bagley in North Shropshire.

Weston Oak, Newcastle-on-Clun. The hollow trunk of the oak housed a postbox, until the tree was felled to accommodate road improvements after the Second World War.

An oak that once stood by the roadside between Clun and Newcastle near the turning to Weston was the appropriately named **'Weston Oak'**. The tree was well known in the area as a valuable landmark on the B4368. It was more important to locals for the fact that within its hollow trunk it housed a postbox. Photographs exist showing the postmen emptying the box.

A local story tells that one winter in heavy snow a horse-drawn hearse carrying a coffin was delayed near the tree as nightfall was approaching. For shelter the coffin was placed into the hollow tree for the night. Next day conditions improved and the hearse and coffin completed their journey to Clun.

The Weston Oak was unfortunately felled in the 1950s to make way for road improvements. A portion of the tree is to be seen in Clun Museum.

Another famous old oak that is no longer with us was the **Shelton Oak**. This tree was also known as 'Glendower's Oak' after a legend connected with the Battle of Shrewsbury in 1403. The Welsh leader Owain Glendwyr reputedly used the oak as a lookout to observe the movements and engagements of the battle at what is now appropriately called Battlefield.

This would seem highly unlikely as the position of the tree at Shelton near the Welshpool road could not possibly have given a view of the battle. There is also conflicting and much stronger evidence to show that Glendwyr was in South Wales at the time. Some historians have also expressed doubt as to whether the tree would have been in existence in 1403.

Strongly supporting the argument that the tree would have been in existence in the early part of the fifteenth century is a document which was found amongst title deeds of a family named Waring. This document belonged to Mad Jack Mytton and was entitled *How the Grette Oake at Shelton standeth on my ground* and was signed by Adam Waring in 1543. Apparently in the document Waring's tenant at Shelton spoke of a "grette oake". There were detailed descriptions of hedgerows all in relationship to the big tree. Also, significantly, there was no reference to the Glendwyr legend which must have come at a later date.

Measured in 1810 by Mr. Parkes for the *Gentlemen's Magazine* the girth of the Shelton Oak at 1.52 metres (5 feet) was 7.64 metres (25 feet 1 inch.) William Phillips measured it in 1879 as 2.33 metres (29 feet). It was then hollow, and the floor was laid with pebbles. It was said that it could take a dozen people standing up and that half a dozen could dine within — I wonder if they tried?

In the 1840s a tenant from Shelton Hall kept a large bear chained to the tree. The bear used the hollow tree for its den. Props were put under the branches and an iron band was placed around the trunk. It was then just alive, showing a few leaves each year.

The tree finally died during the middle of this century but was left as a curiosity. Hatton Gardner wrote in 1946 that it was covered in ivy which he blamed for finally killing the tree. At 1.52 metres (5 feet) he measured the girth at 8.38 metres (27 feet 6 inches) considerably less than Phillips' measurement in 1879! Despite these inaccuracies and inconsistencies one can say that the Shelton Oak was probably in excess of six hundred years old.

The dead tree was finally removed in the 1950s to make way for road improvements. A young oak sapling has been planted as a memorial and stands by the junction of the A5 and Welshpool road.

Several trees grown from acorns of the original Shelton Oak exist, with one

The Shelton Oak (Glendower's Oak) with a written history going back to 1543 received much attention in the Victorian period. This old wood print was featured in the Gardeners Chronicle of 1890.

apparently growing in the Dingle in Shrewsbury.

An oak which had a mysterious story associated with it was the **Brewers Oak.** This tree no longer exists but close to where it originally stood near to the A5 on the north side of Shifnal stands Brewers Oak Farm. Brewer apparently was the name of the man who farmed the land in about 1780. The land on the other side of Watling Street was owned by the Duke of Sutherland and on it stood a big oak tree which the Duke wished to fell for timber. Brewer objected strongly to this and to protect the tree he offered to buy the land for an artificially high figure. The transaction was duly completed and the oak finally belonged to Brewer.

Local people talked of Brewer's obsession with the oak and strange powers were attributed to it. One story tells that Brewer committed suicide by hanging himself from the tree. Another account said the tree held a secret about Brewer which eventually led to his suicide.

Brewer's gravestone has, interestingly, never been found so he may have committed suicide. Another curious fact was that the tree was supposed to have had a strange withered limb but unfortunately the full story appears to have been lost in time. The mystery remains; all that is left is the name of the farm "Brewers Oak".

An oak which existed in Chester Road, Shrewsbury in the 19th century was the **Broad Oak**. Not much is known about the tree apart from its large size. A pencil drawing exists of the tree by Philip Van Dyck Brown (1801-1868). The original now hangs in the Lower Nupend Gallery in Cradley near Malvern.

At another locality in Shrewsbury, the area known as Mytton Oak, there must have been a tree at some time past probably named after Mad Jack Mytton, the famous Shropshire character. The eccentric Shrewsbury M.P. used to live at Mytton Villa, the old 18th century town house located down Mytton Oak Road.

Shropshire's only **Gospel Oak** is found at High Ercall. This tree was used by Methodists as a preaching site from early in the 19th century until about 1855 when the practice was discontinued.

The followers of Methodism were at the time forbidden to hold services in their own houses by the local landowner and there was no land available for them to build a chapel. So open air services were conducted beneath the tree.

This fascinating account relates worship to trees in no uncertain fashion. Deprived of indoor facilities for worship these people were in sense back in primitive times once more and predictably they chose a tree to worship under.

The custom of hanging convicts from 'gallows trees' was the practice in most localities from the Middle Ages through until even the 19th century in some places. A glance at old field names and place names on maps often reveals the spot where either a tree or later a constructed gallows stood. The special tree chosen was generally a sturdy oak with a convenient branch at the right height.

The practice of leaving the body to hang or 'gibbeting', that is nailing the body to the tree as an example to the community and casual passers-by was a common and grisly spectacle. There are two notable cases in Shropshire.

In 1533 an Irishman travelling near Prees Heath was robbed and murdered by a local man named Richard Clowes. Clowes was arrested, tried and hung on the 25th March, 1583 and his body was gibbeted for all to see on an oak tree at Prees Higher Heath. The spot where the tree stood was known from then until now as Gallows Tree Bank.

Located near the Horseshoes Inn on the A5 between Telford and Shrewsbury was the tree once known as **The Gibbet Oak**.

The exact position of the tree is not clear, and whether any one of the oaks still standing near the inn is the original tree cannot be determined. It seems unlikely that the original tree still exists because although the oaks are of some age it is very doubtful that they would have been sufficiently large on 4th September, 1723 to act as gallows. This was the date when the notorious Bolas brothers were hung and gibbetted at this locality. As was the custom they were nailed to the tree and their bodies were left until they literally fell off the tree in pieces.

A report from 1814 on this gruesome event tells of the nails from which the rotting bodies were hung still visible in the trunk of the oak.

A famous old tree that grows near Quatford, south of Bridgnorth on the east side of the Severn is the **Forest Oak**.

In 1082 Roger de Montgomery, a relation of William the Conquerer and one of the major Norman lords of the region, married his second wife Adelissa, who was the daughter of Edward de Pusey one of France's chief nobles.

When Lady Adelissa was sailing to England to join her husband the ship on which she was sailing was engulfed in a dreadful storm. All the crew and passengers believed that the ship would go down and that everybody on board would surely be drowned. During the storm a monk who was travelling with

An old picture depicting the legend of the Forest Oak hangs in Quatford church. The story is also told in the stained glass windows.

Lady Adelissa fell asleep. In his sleep he dreamed that a woman appeared and said to him:-

"If thy Lady would wish to save herself and her attendants from the present danger — let her take a vow to God and faithfully promise to build a church in honour of the Blessed Mary Magdalene on the spot where she may first happen to meet her husband, the earl, in England; especially where groweth a hollow oak and where wild swine have shelter".

When the monk awoke he related his dream to Adelissa and she vowed she would carry out the promise which he related. The storm abated and they completed their crossing without further hazard. Lady Adelissa then travelled to Shropshire.

Riding through the Morfe Forest on top of the sandstone escarpment at Quatford on the edge of the earl's hunting grounds and close by an impressive oak tree Adelissa met Roger who was out hunting boar.

The promise was kept and the building of the church was started on top of the sandstone hill across open land from the oak tree. The church still stands although alterations and additions have been made over the centuries.

This legend is depicted in some 20th century stained glass windows on the south side of the church. The story was first written down during the reign of King John and reference to it hangs in the church.

The Forest Oak which stands today is in fact a 'twin oak' with two trunks. It seems highly unlikely that these two stems could have been in existence since 1082 unless the tree had been one large trunk that has decayed and eventually formed two trunks.

This idea, however tempting would seem improbable. More likely the present Forest Oak could be a replacement planting, although there is no evidence to support this.

This remarkable story is not simply a Victorian romance but is a legend based on fact which has remained unscathed for many centuries.

Two oaks in the region have royal associations and these are part of maybe a hundred or so oaks in Britain that have similar connections with the monarchy.

One of England's most famous trees is the **Royal Oak** at Boscobel near Tong, just inside the county boundary. In fact this tree is of international fame and is visited by thousands of people each year.

The hundreds of public houses named the Royal Oak found throughout England are named after and commemorate the Boscobel oak.

The familiar inn sign depicting the oak and royal crown within its spreading branches originates from the day the future Charles II hid in an oak tree to escape the Parliamentary forces.

The incident happened after Charles had unsuccessfully fought the battle of Worcester and he and his followers fled northwards to escape capture. Dressed as a countryman Charles arrived at White Ladies Priory close to Boscobel House in the early hours of 4th September, 1651. Charles and a friend, Richard Pennderel from Boscobel House, hid amongst the trees in nearby Spring Coppice. The rest of the Royalist party, apart from Lord Wilmot, rode out for Scotland.

The following day Charles and Richard walked nine miles to Madeley with the intention of crossing the River Severn at the ferry below Madeley Bank (the iron bridge was built close by this ferry point in 1779) but they found the river crossings to be well guarded so they spent the day in a barn owned by a Catholic sympathiser named Wolf. That night they returned to Boscobel.

On Saturday, 6th September, 1651, Charles, and a Major Careless who was staying at the house, decided to spend the day in a large oak tree in the nearby Spring Coppice to avoid capture. Charles' account of events was dictated to Samuel Pepys in 1680. Here is an extract:-

"Careless told me it would be dangerous to stay in the house or to go into the wood. He suggested that we climb into a great oak, so that we could see around

Royal Oak, Boscobel.

us, for the enemy would search the wood. I approving, we (that is Careless and I) went and carried up with us some victuals for the whole day viz. bread, cheese, small beer and nothing else and got up into a great oak that had been lopt some three or four years before — and being grown out again very bushy and thick, could not be seen through and here we stayed all day.

Memorandum, That while we were in this tree we see soldiers going up and down, in the thicket of the wood, searching for persons escaped, we seeing them, now and then, peeping out of the wood".

When nightfall came they said they would risk sleeping in the house because the tree was so uncomfortable after so many hours just sitting there. The following two days Charles tried to relax and spent some time in the garden, particularly in the arbor on the mount which is still to be seen at Boscobel today.

He eventually left and made his way via Bristol to Shoreham and sailed to France.

The oak tree in which Charles hid was located about 150 yards south-west of Boscobel House in the woodland known as Spring Coppice. After Charles' triumphant return from France on May 29th, 1660, which initiated the Reformation, the story of the future King and the Boscobel Oak spread quickly and many travellers came to look for the tree and take away souvenirs.

A brick wall was constructed around the tree as protection but the plundering continued so that by 1700 not much of the old tree remained. Many snuff boxes, toys, and even seats were made from the tree and John Evelyn commented that the tree was dead by 1706.

A William Stakeley talked in 1712 of a young sapling oak growing close by the older tree. He assumed it was from an acorn from the Royal Oak. In the 18th century there are several other accounts of two trees. Towards the end of that century only the younger tree is mentioned and there is local evidence the old original tree was dug up. Even the roots were utilised by trophy hunters.

The Victorians pretended that the second tree was in fact the one Charles II hid in. They even changed the descriptive plaques to fit their story. The size of the present tree, although large, indicates an age of about 250/300 years old which is roughly in line with the second tree theory and completely at odds with the description of the Royal Oak that Charles gave.

The original tree from the royal description given was an old thick trunked oak of some fair age that was growing in a coppiced woodland. It had recently been pollarded and was an ideal tree to hide in because of its bushy new growth.

The Royal Oak of today stands in a field, the coppice now cleared. It is surrounded by iron railings put there in 1817. The second tree may have been planted as a replacement tree although no documentary evidence supports this theory. It seems rather a strange coincidence that both the Lady Oak at Cressage and the Royal Oak at Boscobel accidentally grew a young replacement right next to themselves.

There is also a story that states Charles II planted oaks from Boscobel acorns in St. James' Park of London after the Reformation.

There have been numerous paintings, broadsheets, poems and even a coronation medal in 1661 that have added to the fame of the Royal Oak.

The story of the tree that sheltered the future King and allowed him to return as one of the most popular monarchs is now firmly embedded in English history and folklore.

On his triumphant return from France on 29th May, 1660, Charles II named the day Oak Apple Day and decreed that celebrations should commence and that various festivals which had been prohibited by Cromwell's Puritans should be restored.

Strictly speaking the location of **Prince's Oak** near Loton Park is just in Wales but the tree had a close connection with Shropshire.

The tree's fame stems from the fact that in September 1806 the then Prince of Wales (later King George IV) and the Duke of Clarence were staying with Sir Robert Leighton at Loton Hall after visiting Shrewsbury. Sir Robert suggested that the Prince might ride the few hundred yards across the Welsh border so visiting the country for which he was Prince.

This the Prince did and after crossing the border he noticed a majestic oak by the side of the road. He picked some sprigs of foliage from the tree and placing them into his hat rode back to Loton proclaimed he had been to Wales and to prove it he had some Welsh oak in his hat.

From then on the tree was referred to as the Prince's Oak and eventually the locality around the tree assumed this name.

The Prince's Oak is probably more impressive now than it was in 1806. It has a healthy crown of leaves and it stands on top of a bank next to the road. A brick wall and railings have been put around the tree for protection and a descriptive

Prince's Oak, Alberbury – an oak with a story from the early 19th century.

plaque can be found. Nearby the name of the tree is enshrined in the 'place name' road sign.

The wording on the plaque below the tree (as seen on 3rd November, 1985) is as follows:-

> THIS BRASS PLAQUE WAS RESTORED TO THE PRINCE'S OAK IN THE YEAR OF THE CORONATION OF KING GEORGE VI 1937. NEAR THIS TREE HIS ROYAL HIGHNESS THE PRINCE OF WALES WAS INTRODUCED INTO HIS PRINCIPALITY BY SIR RICHARD PULESTON BART ON THE 9TH DAY OF SEPTEMBER 1806.
> PRESENT
> H.R.H. THE DUKE OF CLARENCE, LORD VISCOUNT PETERSHAM, SIR ROBERT LEIGHTON BART, B. FORESTER ESQ., M.P. NOW LORD FORESTER. ROBERT HEATHCOTE ESQ., COLONEL NOW M. GEN'L, SIR BEN BLOOMFIELD AND COL. LEE, 10TH HUSSARS.

The locality of Watch Oak situated on the road from Ironbridge to Atcham (B4380) owes its name to an oak tree that stood in a prominent position beside the old road and a bridleway until 1850 when it reputedly blew down in a gale. The tree which must have commanded a superb view of the Severn Valley towards Shrewsbury was used for such a purpose by Cromwell's troops during the Civil War in the 17th century. The troops were observing the movements of the Royalist supporters.

In later days the Watch Oak was used by people waiting for the stagecoach as it made its way from Shrewsbury, down the old coaching road. An iron plaque that tells the story of the Watch Oak is now fixed to the wall of a cottage called 'The Watch Oak' close to where the tree once stood.

Across the fields south of the Watch Oak stands one of the most impressive spreading oaks that one could ever see. This magnificent tree now called **The Dryton Oak** would make a suitable lookout tree such is the view that can be had from the tree's main fork. The branches of the oak spread across the lane that leads from the B4380 to the Eyton-on-Severn racecourse. The spread of the branches is over 27 metres (90 feet) and the trunk measured 8.43 metres (27 feet 8 inches) in 1983. In the fork is a hole full or rainwater that goes one metre down into the tree. There is no doubt that this tree, if looked after, can become one of Shropshire's great oaks of the future.

An oak growing at the entrance to **Admaston Spa**, near Wellington in Telford was one of many trees planted up and down the country to commemorate the jubilee of Queen Victoria in 1863. The tree is now a fine specimen and in 1985 plans were in hand to have a fence and descriptive plaque erected next to the tree.

So, in Shropshire we have a fine collection of distinguished old oaks as befits an ancient county rich in legend and folklore. There are many other large oak trees of only slightly less physical stature than those described but which have not had the advantage of being highlighted by historical accident.

Chapter 6
The Natives

Certain individuals and groups of trees from the small band of native species that grow in Britain have achieved some fame, in some cases not only in Shropshire but in the country as a whole.

The native black poplar *(Populus Nigra-var, betulifolia)*, uncommon over much of Britain, is found in isolated pockets of Shropshire. There are some excellent specimens in the Severn Valley and surrounding districts. Growing at Leighton Hall, near Buildwas is one of the country's tallest at over 39 metres (123 feet). There are two giants at Longnor Hall, beside the brook within the deer park. One of the trees has a British record girth of over 7·4 metres (24 feet). The other tree is one of the tallest in Britain at 39.5 metres (124 feet). Longnor also has the county girth record for Scots pine at 5 metres (16 feet 3 inches). Another noteworthy black poplar can be found near the village of Stapleton with a girth of 6.4 metres (20 feet 9 inches).

Arbor Tree, Aston-on-Clun, the tree that is decorated with flags every May.

By far the most famous of all black poplars is the **Arbor Tree** of Aston-on-Clun. Standing on raised ground by a bridge over a stream near the centre of the village, this large leafy old hollow tree is, throughout the year, emblazoned with multi-coloured flags attached to long larch poles, which are nailed to its trunk.

Every year on or about Oak Apple Day, the 29th May, the tree is re-dressed with new flags and a unique celebration takes place. A pageant is staged by the villagers which re-enacts an historic wedding procession to the tree. Local children dressed in costume rush up the lane to meet a 'bride and bridegroom' who approach in a pony and trap. The 'villagers' then escort them to the tree. Dancing takes place near the tree and in recent years has included a troupe of girls dressed in white, each carrying a knotted handkerchief of white linen and a small oak bough. Morris dancing follows to conclude the festivities by the tree and a village fete is held in a nearby field.

Twenty-five years ago the pageant was a far more elaborate affair and was a form of history play enacted on a wooden stage under the tree itself. Photographs and reports of the time show that the 'cast' followed a certain historical order beginning in very ancient times.

First to appear was Diana, Goddess of Nature, followed by a Celtic shepherd and his bride. Then came St. George of England and St. George of Ethiopia. Bridget of Kildare preceded a grim Puritan who gave way to Charles II, the Merry Monarch, and lastly there was Squire John Marston and his bride, Mary Carter.

That year the pageant was followed by a ballet troupe, Morris dancing and handbell ringing.

Then, scions (cuttings) taken from the tree were ceremoniously given to brides

Dressing the Arbor Tree, Aston-on-Clun, May 1986.

Black Poplars, Longnor Deer Park. Two trees that have national fame.

who came forward, presumably wishing for fertility. This practice is now discontinued.

In the late 1950s and into the 1960s the ceremony and fete attained the stature of a small festival with a distinctly international flavour. The most remarkable thing though is that such an ancient practice has survived.

It is the only tree dressing ceremony remaining in Britain and as the former pageant suggested the whole ritual has ancient roots in early pagan fertility rites.

The poplar is named "The Arbor Tree' but it also used to be known by its earlier name, 'The Brides Tree'. The word bride is derived from St. Bridget or the even earlier 'Brid' the Celtic fertility goddess. It is known that the Celts would hang articles of women's clothing on special trees to ensure fertility and the practice of hanging objects on trees, a form of votive offering is a worldwide phenomenon continuing to the present day in certain areas. The earliest written records of the Arbor Tree are from the 29th May, 1786 when on that date John Marston from nearby Oaker married Mary Carter of Sibdon.

Several versions of the story exist. They are:-

(a) That on 29th May, 1786 John Marston and Mary Carter married and to celebrate the marriage the tree was decorated with flags.

(b) That on the wedding day Mary Carter on being introduced to the village noticed the tree decorated with flags and so liked them that she contributed to the dressing and annual festivities from that year onwards. A sovereign was given to each villager on the anniversary of the wedding and free food was available for travellers at the local village inn.

(c) That it was John Marston's second marriage, his first had been childless. He took his new bride to the tree because of its supposed powers of fertility for he badly wanted an heir for the Oaker Estate.

It seems that the tree may have worked its magic for Mary had four children in quick succession. Both John and Mary Carter are buried together at Hopesay church. The family tombstone can be seen near the church porch.

In later years the Marston family seemed dogged by bad luck and local stories circulate of the misfortune that started in the Civil War when the massacres at Hopton Castle resulted in a curse being put on all people who took land that had once belonged to those slaughtered.

The Marston family at Oaker suffered tragedies for centuries, eventually ending when the last son in line, who suffered, it is said from melancholia, committed suicide after his wife had left him in the 1950s. Up to that date the Marston family had paid for the dressing of the tree. After that the Oaker Estate

Oak Apple Day, Aston-on-Clun.

broke up and Hopesay Parish Council took over the care of the Arbor Tree. During the early 1950s the ceremony almost disappeared but thanks to the dedicated work of a number of enthusiasts it was kept going. By 1956 it was thriving again and during the late 1970s and 1980s the increasing interest, particularly from young people in traditions and customs, has sustained the revival, and now, as described on 29th May each year a fair with music and dancing follows the tree dressing 'play' that depicts the Marston wedding of 1786.

On the very significant date of 29th May, 1660, Charles II returned to England from France on his birthday to restore not only the monarchy but also the old festivals and customs including the Spring festival that was termed 'Oak Apple Day' or 'Arbor Day'. (Oak apples were placed by doors in Shrewsbury on 29th May up to the 19th century.) These essentially pagan festivals were frowned upon and purged during the 15th and 16th centuries and also during Cromwell's rule. The tree dressing probably continued uninterrupted from 1660 until 1786 when the wedding took place. The Marston connection kept alive the practice and with the support of the Oaker Estate the tree was well looked after until the 1950s.

Considering all the known facts it seems inconceivable that the dressing of this tree began at the time of the Marston wedding in 1786, but it is certainly true that the Marston family helped greatly to perpetuate the practice and it is to this and the efforts of the parish council since 1950 that we owe this valuable glimpse back into a very distant past.

A few questions remain which cannot be answered. If estimates are correct the black poplar was planted around 1700 or thereabouts. Why a black poplar and what did it replace, an oak perhaps?

The Christian Bridget of Kildare, displacing in the pageant the ancient Moon Goddess Diana who with Artemis was the goddess of fertility, is known to have founded a church (it is not known where) near a tree shrine and to have adapted fertility customs to Christianity. Whatever the historical truth, the story of the Arbor Tree fascinates because of its undoubted mythical connections with an ancient past.

We can only guess and seek parallels as to what happened before 1786. What we do know is that the flags still adorn the Abor Tree and long may they do so.

THE BALLAD OF THE ARBOR TREE

In Aston Clun stands a tree
A poplar dressed like a ship at sea
Lonely link with an age long past;
of Arbor Trees I am the last.

Since seventeen eighty-six my day
is writ the twenty ninth of May
When new flags fly and we rejoice,
New life has stilled harsh winter's voice.

To greet a Squire's lovely bride
Did tenants dress my boughs with pride?
But old wives say, my flags are worn
To mark the day an heir was born.

Wise men mellow o'er evening ale
Old feuds and wicked deeds retail.
Thanksgiving dressed my arms they say
For peace when blood feuds died away.

Did hear! My father mark the rite
of Shepherds gone with world's first light?
Was England merrie neath his shade
Till crop-haired Cromwell joy forbade?

In sixteen sixty with the Spring
Came merry Charles the exiled King.
Did he proclaim May twenty-nine
"Arbor Day" for revelry and wine?

And Shepherds plagued with pox and chills
Turn to the old ways of the hills,
To "Mystic Poplar" to renew
Fertility in field and ewe?

Stand I for Ancient ways, for birth,
For love, for peace, for joy and mirth?
Riddle my riddle as you will
I stand for good and not for ill.

And if my dress your fancy please
Help my flags to ride the breeze
That you with me will in the sun,
Welcome all, to the Vale of Clun.

Tom Beardsley, Clun.

Another native species of tree well worth looking out for is the wild service tree *(Sorbus torminalis)* a most interesting member of the Sorbus family that is sometimes called the 'Checkers Tree'.

The service tree is normally found in old woodlands and if found today is a good indicator that the area has been continuously wooded since medieval times at least. The wild service is occasionally found in hedgerows down country lanes. Several trees growing near a stream at Hughley are supposed to have been planted as boundary markers. There are also old examples in the Church Stretton area. At Edgmond near Newport down Robin Hood Road can be found one of the county's largest service trees. Another hedgerow example is at Hopton Cangeford near Cuckoopen Coppice.

Another tree associated with ancient woodland sites is the small leaved lime *(Tilia cordata)* and there are many examples of this beautiful tree in the county.

The largest one in the county is at Oakly Park, Bromfield which has a girth of 5.44 metres (17 feet 10 inches).

The large-leaved lime *(Tilia platyphyllos)* is probably another native lime, but only to the limestone soils of the Wye Valley and south Yorkshire. It has been much planted as a street tree and in municipal parks, where avenues of these attractive trees are common throughout England. The excellent limes planted along the footpaths in the Quarry at Shrewsbury belong to this species. They are not though the original trees, but are replacements. An extract from *Shropshire Folk-lore* describes the Quarry and the planting of the original trees thus:-

"In former times it (the Park) was used for games, open air plays so forth; but in the year 1719 the Corporation determined to lay it out and plant it with trees for a public promenade. One Wright, a famous nurseryman of those days, living at Bicton, was employed, and about 400 trees, more or less, were planted, which now form beautiful shady avenues by the riverside. Such are the facts; Now for the alternative story:-

Thomas Wright was a famous nurseryman in the old days. He had made a large fortune by his trade and wished to spend some of it in benefiting the town of Shrewsbury. He therefore proposed to plant the Quarry with trees, but the Mayor and Corporation were old-fashioned people and refused to allow any change to be made. But Wright would not be gainsaid. He was a man who knew more than most people and understood a good deal about conjuring and that sort of thing. He was determined that the Quarry should be planted and by means of his magic he managed, with only two men to help him, to plant all the trees in a single night, and when the Mayor got up in the morning the thing was done. But even he was obliged to own up that the work was a great improvement and it was therefore allowed to remain".

These original limes were condemned as dangerous in 1949 and felled.

In Europe, particularly Germany, are found some very old large-leaved limes, usually in the squares of medieval towns. Some of these trees are known to be in excess of seven hundred years old. In England big old limes are not so commonly found. Nevertheless in Shropshire we are fortunate in having the largest, and oldest, large-leaved lime in Britain. This is the **Pitchford Lime** located, within the grounds of Pitchford Hall, near Acton Burnell. This superb Tudor building with its intricate timber work was built around 1560 for the Ottley family, although there is evidence of an earlier structure.

Written on an old Pitchford Hall estate map of 1692 are the words "The tree with the house in it". This makes the lime certainly over four hundred years old as it seems obvious that the tree must have been fairly large to have accommodated the tree house at that time.

The impressive tree stands on high ground to the south-west of the Hall.

The tree house, which is now a black and white timbered structure, has had several alterations carried out to it over the centuries. In the 1970s it was completedly renovated and extensive propping of the tree with metal supports was carried out. Inside the tree house there is ornate plaster work. Extensive tree surgery work was also carried out at the same time. A timber staircase takes you up to the tree house and a fine view can be observed from the windows.

The young Queen Victoria, when staying at Pitchford Hall in her childhood,

Dovaston Yew, West Felton. The original tree planted in 1777 still grows at John Dovaston's old nursery site near the A5.

kept a diary of the events and she mentioned visiting the tree house on the 28th October, 1832.

28th October, 1832

"I awoke at seven and got up at half-past seven. At half-past nine we breakfasted. After breakfast I drew and at eleven went to church. At a little past one we came home and walked about the grounds, and I went up a staircase to a little house in a tree."

This tree and house are unique to Britain. It is undoubtedly the best tree house we have and one of the best in the world. The idea to construct it may have come from family travels in Europe.

Another notable feature of the Pitchford Lime is the prolific growth of mistletoe adorning its branches. Old limes are a favourite place for mistletoe to grow but the Pitchford tree has a particularly large collection of this unusual plant.

The field maple *(Acer campestre)* is our native member of the Acer family and it grows freely in hedges and on the edge of woodland. It never grows to the size of the more common, but introduced, sycamore but it is an attractive tree with superb, butter yellow foliage in the Autumn. A good size bole on a field maple is around 2 metres (6 feet 6 inches). One found between Shrawardine and Pentre has a girth of 2.4 metres (7 feet 9 inches) and is over 15 metres (48 feet 9 inches) tall.

The sad story of the disappearing elm is well known and only a few examples of the English elm *(Ulmus procera)* are left in Shropshire hedgerows. The regrowth tree from the stumps of felled trees though may provide some hope for the future. The woodland home of the Wych Elm *(Ulmus glabra)* ensures greater protection from Dutch elm disease and there are still some very large specimens especially along the Severn Valley.

There are many different varieties of ornamental cherries but the native cherry is called the Gean *(Prunus avium)*. Covered in a May shower of pure white blossom it can be found in hedgerows along woodland edges and glades. Of the many examples of this tree in Shropshire the largest are the 2.4 metres (7 feet 10 inches) girthed tree at Apley Castle, Telford, and the 3 metres (9 feet 9 inches) girthed tree at Bromley Hall.

A tree which has many connections with countryside traditions is the hawthorn *(Crataegus monogyna)*. The May Queen of pagan England was crowned with May blossom and the month of May takes its name from the blossom that used to flower during the old calendar month of May (changed 1751) that commenced ten days later than the present month.

The story of the Winter flowering Glastonbury Thorn, reputedly planted by Joseph of Arimathea, is an interesting legend associated with the hawthorn. There are of course many thorns growing in hedgerows and scrubland but the rarer Midland thorn *(Crataegus oxycantha)* is a tree of the woods and shade. A very large hawthorn can be seen at Marche Manor with a girth of over 2 metres (6 feet 6 inches).

Pitchford Lime and Tree House.

Britain has only four truly native evergreens, the holly, the juniper, the yew and the Scots pine. The Scots pine is our only native member of the pine family; the yew seems indestructable and prolific in Shropshire, the juniper, native to the chalk downlands, is in serious decline nationally. Linked so closely with Christmas time, the remaining native evergreen, the holly, has a well-established presence in hedgerows and woodlands throughout the country.

The 'Hollies' is not an uncommon place-name in the west of the country and in Shropshire it is found in various locations. Around the Stiperstones area, which was once the Stiperstones Forest are several places called 'Hollies'. One of particular interest is at Lords Hill on the north side of the Stiperstones above Snailbeach, here, on the ridge, are some old holly trees (150/200) scattered about the hillside. Many of the trees have fallen and are in an advanced state of decay. Others lean, their old trunks gnarled and contorted into strange sculptured shapes. Out of many of these trees grow younger rowans that have seeded into the broken forks and split trunks of the hollies. They have survived there because they are safe from the sheep which eat everything growing at ground level.

There are various theories as to the origins of this 'holly forest'; the most convincing of which is that the hollies are survivors from the edge of an extensive oakwood that once grew there. In fact it is known that a particularly large old oak used to grow amongst them.

Holly is a common understory tree of both oakwoods and beechwoods. At the edge of these woods it can become a prolific seedling tree and in some rare cases, normally at fairly high elevations, it can form almost pure holly woods. One of the most well known can be found above the Upper Lakes at Killarney in

Modern drawing of Pitchford Lime and Tree House.

Ireland. The stems of these high hollies are often silvery grey, almost white, unlike the darker bark of the lowland trees.

It was the practice in the Welsh border lands from the Middle Ages onwards to use holly foliage for winter livestock fodder. In the poorer hill districts wooden 'mashers' were used to crush the leaves to make them more edible. It is interesting to find that the lower leaves of holly have prickles, whilst those above the browsing line do not. Is this a form of evolutionary defence?

Like all the native evergreens the holly is steeped in superstition. The pagan song the 'holly' boy and 'ivy' girl was originally sung on Shrove Tuesday and it is still considered unlucky to fell a holly tree and many are left for that reason in hedgerows. This superstition may have helped the survival of the Lords Hill hollies. At old fairs and markets alcohol was often sold by or under a holly bush as part of early licensing arrangements and the pub name 'Hollybush' may signify a location where such a bush stood. The hollies at Lords Hill are well worth visiting as they create a rare and unique landscape.

In the last few years several areas of the Hill have been fenced off to keep livestock out so as to encourage regeneration of the holly wood. It is hoped that this will be beneficial otherwise the hollies will no doubt disappear.

An unusual evergreen which grows within Shropshire at the old nursery at West Felton is the **Dovaston** or **Weeping Yew**. The tree is an excellent specimen with a spread of over 20 metres (65 feet). The trunk is screened by pendulous hanging branchlets which are its distinctive feature. This tree is of great botanical interest in that it was only the third specimen planted in Britain and the oldest surviving one. The West Felton tree was planted in 1777 by John Dovaston who bought it from a local pedlar. The tree is male, apart from one female branch which bears berries.

John Dovaston (1740-1808) was a self-educated man, noted for his ingenuity and energy. He acquired mechanical knowledge and planned and built the nursery complete with a saw mill. His great interest was tree planting and he enthusiastically filled the gardens of his home and the nursery with exotic trees. When the Shropshire Archaeological Society visited the nursery on their annual expedition of 1805, the grounds were reported as having "trees representative of every country of the world".

John Dovaston's son J. T. Milward Dovaston, although educated at Oswestry and Shrewsbury and trained as a barrister, preferred to live at the nursery devoting himself to his great interests, poetry and nature. He died unmarried and the nursery passed to a nephew, whose grandson emigrated to New Zealand in the 1960s. Many of the old trees in the nursery were tragically damaged by fire in the 1960s and the house is now in ruins. The remaining garden is a tangle of neglected trees and undergrowth in which grow an Oriental plane and a Monkey Puzzle. The celebrated Dovaston Yew is protected by a Tree Preservation Order.

The publication *A Flora of Shropshire* by W. A. Leighton, published by John Davies in 1841, describes the planting and development of the Dovaston or Weeping Yew and a list of people to whom seedlings were sent.

The ash is a common tree of Shropshire and many fine examples can be found around the county.

An interesting story concerning an old ash tree that incorporates fact and legend is recounted in the Bridgnorth area.

The Hollies, Lords Hill, Snailbeach – tough survivors growing high in the Shropshire hills.

Common Beech, Hawkstone Park. A magnificent specimen of this noble tree.

Beech Avenue, Linley Hill. A well known landscape feature in south Shropshire.

On Wednesday 26th November, 1912, a miller named Wiggins was returning to his home at Eardington, two miles from Bridgnorth, after working at Wolverhampton market. The time was between 6 p.m. and 7 p.m. About a mile from his home he was set upon by a robber. Wiggins resisted the attack, the assailant drew a pistol and shot Wiggins below the heart.

He then ran off penniless being pursued by the shot man for about 100 yards.

After Wiggins had fallen, somebody from the nearby turnpike house heard his cries and helped him into the house, but Wiggins soon died.

At the spot where Wiggins fell was an old ash tree and the site became notorious as a haunted spot. On the ash tree around a hole in the trunk there was it was said a red blood mark in the shape of a cross, and each year on the anniversary of his death locals would gather to see the tree and 'Blood stain'.

Wiggins' murderer was never caught and the old ash named **Wiggins Tree** was felled after the Second World War to make way for a road improvement scheme.

It is not known if many stories or legends exist in which the Scots pine figures. However a notable exception is found in the case of the **Bryneddin Pine.**

Near the village of Chapel Lawn in South Shropshire can be found the old hanging oak wood known as Bryneddin Wood.

Growing high up on the steep south-facing slope of the valley amidst the fresh green oaks stands a solitary dark Scots pine, forming a curious dark spot on the hillside.

From the opposite hilltop of 'Caer Caradoc', the Iron Age Hill Fort casts a long shadow over Bryneddin Wood. On the shortest day of the year (the Winter Solstice), December 21st betweeen 3 p.m. and 4 p.m., the shadow of the Hill Fort just touches the pine.

It is not known who planted the tree, but it is likely that it was planted early this century. Thus the story behind this inspired piece of planting will probably remain a mystery.

The present pattern of ownership of this almost pure oak wood dates from the medieval period. Villagers still own strips of the wood originally defined by meer stones running parallel up the hill side, although the old woodland management practices have long since gone.

Because only a few of these meer stones can now be found, the precise boundaries of individual ownership have become blurred and indistinct.

Running along the foot of the hillside an old communal track, used for carting out timber which had been cut and thrown down the slope, can still be found. This is called a 'rack'. Another 'rack' now simply a footpath, cuts a straight rising diagonal through the wood from bottom west to top east. Just below this 'rack', near the eastern end, can be found the Pine.

Bryneddin Pine, with the hill fort of Caer Caradoc, Chapel Lawn, in the background.

Chapter 7
The Introduced Trees

Before and during the medieval period there were only a few introductions of new trees, shrubs and other plants into the British Isles. Although it has been proved that it is possible to grow a wide range of tree in Britain, it is a relatively unrealised fact that, prior to the medieval period, the range of native tree species was remarkably small.

Main native species
Alder, ash, beech, birch, box, hazel, holly, lime, oak, pine, yew, hawthorn, hornbeam, elms.

Other natives
Crab apples, gean and bird cherry, juniper, field maple, poplars, rowan, whitebeam, wild service, willows.

Native shrubs
Alder buckthorn, barberry, blackthorn, buckthorn, broom, dogwood, elder, guelder rose, gorse, privet, rose, sea buckthorn, spindle, wayfaring tree.

The species that were first introduced were principally brought in by the herbalists, most of whom were monks, and, slowly, over a period of time, these non-native species began to influence what could be grown and seen in Britain. These early introductions were simply plants that were considered to be important either as a source of food or for medical purposes. The Romans though are credited with bringing several tree species to Britain. The most well known being the sweet chestnut *(Castanea sativa)* and the sycamore *(Acer pseudoplatanus)*. The sweet chestnut is a long lived tree and many huge examples

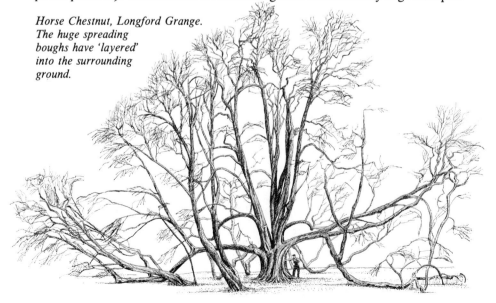

Horse Chestnut, Longford Grange. The huge spreading boughs have 'layered' into the surrounding ground.

Cedar of Lebanon, Acton Burnell Castle – a dramatic setting for this solitary tree.

can be found in England on old estates and parkland. There are some impressive examples at Croft Castle in Herefordshire but the most notable specimen is near Tortworth church in Gloucestershire. In Shropshire there are large trees at Grinshill, Kinlet and Shotton Hall. Although the last example has suffered from lightning damage in recent years.

The well known sycamore, often maligned by conservationists, is of course extremely common everywhere. It is at its best when growing singly in open parkland. Then it can grow a huge spreading crown and in old age its bark can take on attractive hues especially when complemented by early Spring or Autumnal leaf colouring. There are many specimens in Shropshire with girth measurements of over 4 metres (13 feet) but excellent trees can be found at

Ornamental Trees, Millechope Park. The classic places to see the trees of the world are the gardens and parks of the big houses and estates.

Sheriffhales, Apley Park (Bridgnorth), Wroxeter, Loton Park and two at Halston, one with a branch spread of over 48 metres (156 feet). The county's best known Sycamore used to stand at Loton Park and was held together with ironwork. It finally fell apart in a severe storm in the 1950s. The old stump is still visible in the garden near the hall.

Between 1600 and 1700 some American species arrived, brought by the traders who visited that continent.

Notable introductions included the tulip tree, false acacia or locust tree, swamp cypress, scarlet oak and the Canadian spruces. The two great tulip trees of Shropshire are the specimen at Dale End Park, Ironbridge and the older, bigger but less healthy tree at the old vicarage, Highley. This tree is probably in excess of 200 years old but is younger than the 17th century mansion beside it. There are several fine examples of young tulip trees decorating Shrewsbury's streets.

The opening of trade routes to the Near East and the Orient began to bring in further species such as the well-known tree, the horse chestnut, such a common sight in English parkland, which came from Greece and Albania early in the 17th century. There is an unusually fine Shropshire example at Longford Grange, near Lilleshall which holds the county girth record for this species of 6.5 metres (21 feet). This well developed tree, which has an outer ring of 'layered' branches, is 33 metres (107 feet 3 inches) in height and has a crown which measures 40 metres (130 feet) across.

The Cedar of Lebanon is a species which was planted adjacent to many 18th century country houses. The first was brought from Mount Lebanon in 1646; the original tree still stands near Wantage, Oxfordshire. A very fine Shropshire example, which well illustrates the cult of the specimen tree on the lawn, can be found at Rowton Castle, on the Shrewsbury/Welshpool road. This is a really magnificent specimen with a height of over 30 metres (97 feet 6 inches) and a crown measuring 40 metres (133 feet) across. The girth is 9.75 metres (31 feet 8 inches) making this one of the country's largest cedars. Another superb specimen stands next to the ruins of Acton Burnell Castle. The tree is exceptionally tall with branches spreading over the castle remains. There can be few more dramatic locations than where this cedar grows.

The familiar London plane, first planted at Ely Cathedral in 1680 and still surviving, was another useful addition to planting schemes.

This is the commonest tree found in London squares, hence its name. There are several fine examples in Shropshire notably at Burford and Millechope, but the ones seen by many visitors to Shropshire are the lines of trees at Smithfield Road, Shrewsbury and Coalport High Street. Even more well known are the two towering plane trees in St. Mary's Churchyard, Shrewsbury.

During the early part of the 18th century tree introductions began in earnest and 'immigrants' such as the European larch and the Norway spruce were planted on an ever-increasing scale, gradually assuming great economic importance as timber trees.

In Scotland, at Dunkeld and Blair Castle can be found the first larches, now huge, which were originally planted in 1738 and 1780 respectively, these being the very first larches ever to be brought into this country.

In Shropshire, at Linley Hall, near Bishop's Castle, still stand some of

England's first larch trees. The then owner of Linley Hall, Robert Moore, a distinguished traveller and naturalist, knew the famous botanist, Linneus, and had the larches planted by a stream in a sheltered valley by the house in about 1750. One of the largest of these trees fell in 1954; it was (41.5 metres) 135 feet tall. The county possesses other impressive larches, the one at Mawley Hall, near Cleobury Mortimer, being amongst the largest.

Also, by the early 18th century, the great English landscaped parks had begun to be laid out, many of the older parks being 'improved' and altered; artificial lakes, grottoes, walks, drives and new plantations were created. Thus the classic English parkland, complete with its deer herd and specimen trees, began to appear.

Later in the century the 'pleasure ground' and the arboretum became fashionable. Forerunners of the public park these were places where people of leisure could walk and admire the introduced so-called 'ornamental' trees which were usually planted in front of a backcloth of native species.

Although native to the southern counties of Britain the beech was a tree frequently used for this purpose because of its magnificent form.

Up the side of Linley Hill, near Linley Hall in Shropshire, is an early beech avenue, planted it is thought after the Napoleonic Wars by unemployed ex-soldiers. The older trees are now dying off but later plantings have maintained this impressive and historic landscape feature. The avenue shows on Baugh's map of Shropshire in 1808, so part of the avenue or a previous one probably predates the Napoleonic Wars.

Landscape designers, on the grand scale, such as Kent, 'Capability' Brown and Repton, incorporated timber production into their designs and a great

Cedar of Lebanon, Rowton Castle. The huge spread makes this cedar one of the most spectacular trees in the county.

Aerial photograph of The Hollies showing the scattered trees on the hillside. 150/200 remain from the original more extensive wood.

Old burry Elm, near Ford. Alas a rare sight since the ravages of elm disease in the 1970s.

Tree landscape, Kingsland House. The combination of deciduous and conifer gives colour to the setting, especially in autumn. Photo: K. Dodwell.

Autumn in Shrewsbury. Horse Chestnut, Kingsland.

Photo:
K. Dodwell.

number of small coverts and tree clumps now a familiar sight, originated during this innovative period of landscape development. Attingham Park, near Shrewsbury, was laid out by Repton in 1798. It is now owned by the National Trust and can be visited at most times of the year.

The final long list of 18th century plant introductions include such well-known trees as the copper beech, manna ash, weeping willow, turkey oak, paperbark birch and Corsican pine.

The steady trickle of plant introductions during the 18th century became, by the early 19th, a flood. In 1810 Kew Gardens, which was first created in 1759, already had a collection of 11,000 species and this total increased rapidly thereafter. In addition to new species from overseas, botanists and nurserymen were at work selecting and crossing both new and old material.

During the 19th century professional plant hunters were sent out to all parts of the globe by botanic gardens, nurseries and private patrons in search of new and exotic species. One of the most famous was David Douglas whose intrepid adventures have now become part of our tree folklore. His encounters with hostile Indians and with bears and his fight against illness and failing eyesight provide a strange commentary to the apparently gentle art of plant hunting. The loss of four years of valuable notes whilst negotiating rapids and his tragic end by being gored to death in a wild bull pit in Hawaii are all part of the vivid Douglas story.

His name is enshrined in the Douglas Fir, one of the world's greatest timber trees. An original, grown from the first imported seed, still stands at Walcot Park, near Bishop's Castle. Another Douglas fir at Walcot Park, planted slightly later than this original tree, is considered to be one of the country's finest examples of this species.

The classic age of the conifer was during the middle of the 19th century with the spectacular discovery of the American big trees, such as sitka spruce, western hemlock, western red cedar the giant redwoods and many others.

Many pinetum were created in the mid-1800s such as Bedgebury in Kent which now contains the national collection of conifers.

The rapid growth in the number of new gardens and parks during the 19th century was a sign of a new interest in botany and horticulture and in Victorian and Edwardian times introductions continued apace; the Japanese cherries being brought in during this period as part of the intense European interest in Japanese art and culture in the late 1800s.

Also since 1847 when the Towns Improvement Clauses Act first empowered local authorities amongst other things to spend money on tree planting, there has been increasing public involvement in this sphere supported by a general consensus of opinion that the presence of trees is an essential part of a good environment. These public plantings also brought new species to the general public's attention.

When looking at the landscape today, it is difficult to find places where introduced tree species cannot be seen, such is the impact of their widespread use.

From large estates, forestry plantations through public parks, town streets, to private suburban gardens, trees, shrubs and plants from almost all over the world now form an integral part of the everyday scene.

Chapter 8
The Future

We are perhaps fortunate in these Islands to be able to grow trees from an extremely wide spectrum of the world's climatic zones. Thus some of the greatest collections of trees are in Britain and each county has its notable collections. (See map and lists.)

There are no doubt many more fine Shropshire trees that deserve to be mentioned in this book standing unfound in various corners of the county. Trees do not have to have stories or legends attached to them to make them interesting. Neither do they have to be the oldest or biggest of their species. A walk or drive around Shropshire will reveal many trees that are both pleasing to the eye and provide a worthwhile function be it shade, ornament or standing timber.

In this publication we have deliberately concentrated on individual trees rather than the 'natural' place for tree growth — the woodland. Woodlands are a subject in themselves and they must be seen as a complete entity in their own right, a living system that in most of lowland Britain is the climax vegetation. If we gave up agriculture, gardening and building the county would soon turn into wildwood again.

There is at present particular concern for our ancient semi-natural woodlands. These are the areas of land that have had managed woodland upon them since before the Middle Ages. This continuous woodland cover has allowed an extremely rich flora and fauna to develop and losses of these beautiful woodlands have been particularly acute over the last few decades. The woods have either been felled and ploughed up or felled and planted with fast growing conifers. Once the woodland 'system' has been destroyed it cannot be recreated.

The practice of 'coppicing' woodland though must not be seen as destruction. Coppicing means cutting down regrowth to the 'stools' or stumps on a cycle and allowing the tree to send up fresh shoots. This practice was the commonest system of woodland management in Britain up until last century. There is now a great deal of interest and information available on coppicing for those who wish to find out more.

On a global scale the tree situation is bleak, with the increasing destruction of the tropical rain forests continuing despite the knowledge that the long term effects of such actions could be disastrous. In many African and Asian countries the clearance of tree cover is breaking down the delicate ecological balance so leading in some places to the creation of dustbowls. The result is often poverty and famine that brings not only untold suffering but also helps to cripple the economies of poor communities.

In the northern more industrialised countries wide scale pollution of the atmosphere and the resulting acid rain threatens thousands of hectares of Europe's natural forests and plantations. There is of course no quick simple solution to these problems but one must always be on the look-out for the origins of potential danger. The large scale movement of timber around the globe can transmit harmful diseases to fresh continents. The lessons of Dutch elm disease should not be forgotten.

Deodar Cedar, Walcot Park. This Himalayan cedar is one of the many fine trees to be found at Walcot.

Weeping Beech, Hodnet Hall. Hodnet has some excellent trees and shrubs set in beautiful gardens.

Giant London Plane, Burford House. Photo: K. Dodwell.

Nevertheless these subjects are now being discussed openly and if irrational prejudices and destructive attitudes can be removed then progress in the right direction can be made.

On the smaller more local scale, where probably major change starts, there are encouraging signs with the renewed interest in woodland management and the development of new versions of the old techniques in, for example, the construction industry. This may give home-grown hardwood a greater economic role in the future. Improved and more generous grants are now available particularly for the growing of broad-leaved trees. Voluntary groups are expanding and becoming better organised, informed and trained. In Shropshire some 'pioneer' schemes have been started and the use of 'green' unseasoned wood is being put to traditional and modern uses. Professional advice, grant aid and administrative backing is there; it now requires people on the ground to either provide or develop the necessary practical skills necessary to plant, maintain and manage trees and woodlands.

With over 90 percent of all our current timber needs coming from abroad surely it makes sense to try and develop our own production and if we want broad-leaved woodlands, to create new markets. The farming community are already aware that they are going to have to look at other sorts of land use in the future.

Returning to the individual tree, many of the ones mentioned in this book are remnants from the time when such trees were important to the local community. They were looked after because they supplied necessary resources and only incidentally because they happened to appeal to the human aesthetic sense. Used they certainly were, especially the old pollard oaks, that formed an essential part of the rural economy because of the valuable produce. When trees are no longer part of that rural economy they become vulnerable.

In the countryside trees in the form of woodlands and shelterbelts still have a value in terms of the shelter they provide, especially in exposed areas. They can of course change the micro-climate of an area allowing crops and plants to be grown which would not otherwise flourish.

In towns and suburbs trees have been recognised since at least the Victorian times for the beauty they provide and for the 'civilising' effect they have on the urban scene. Indeed in some fortunate towns the amount of woodland, the diversity of habitat and the consequent richness of the wildlife generated can often outstrip that of the surrounding agricultural countryside.

On the other hand it is now impossible to see and difficult to imagine what the native tree cover was originally like.

In can be argued that variety has brought benefits. Contrary to what may be sometimes said, some of the more 'exotic ornamentals' can provide habitats for wildlife. Birds, for example, make use of conifers in mixed plantations for Winter cover and for nest protection in the Spring. Variety in tree and shrub cover may well encourage variety in wildlife in certain cases. Although their selection and planting needs careful thought and planning.

Most trees have a longer life span than our own and that factor links us with the past and forward to the future, so widening our horizons. A tree can give a sense of stability and continuity. The great landscape designers never saw their work reach maturity but we have. The forester who plants now for the next generation is an example of the continuity which we should be a part of.

If in this publication we have whetted your appetite to learn more about trees and their surroundings, if you start looking at trees with a new or fresh interest, then we have succeeded.

Tulip tree, Dale End, Ironbridge. A unique tree from the U.S.A. growing in the attractive and popular park near the River Severn.

Douglas Fir, Walcot Park, grown from the original seed sent to Britain by the great plant collector, David Douglas, in 1827.

Fern Leafed Beech, Loton Park. An unusual form of the Common Beech. This tree is gradually reverting back to the original foliage so both leaves are visible on the same branches.

Silver Maple, Youth Hostel, Coalbrookdale. A tree much planted in recent years but not many mature trees can be found locally.

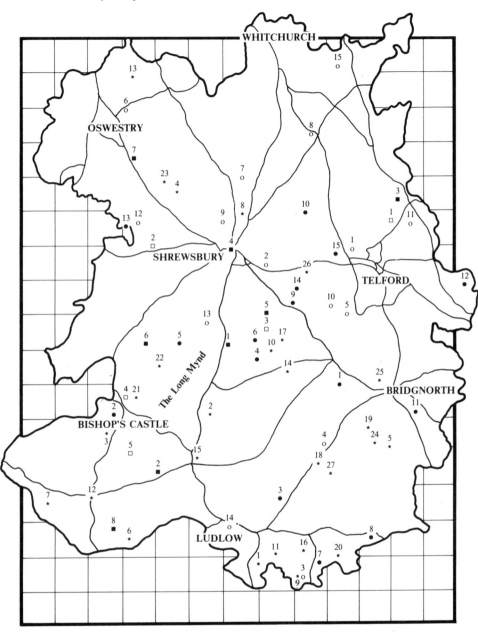

Key:

★ Largest Churchyard Yews   ■ Natives   O Notable Collections

● Oaks   □ Introduced

★ Largest Churchyard Yews
1. Ashford Carbonnel
2. Acton Scott
3. Bishop's Castle
4. Baschurch
5. Billingsley
6. Bucknell
7. Bettws-y-crwyn
8. Battlefield
9. Burford
10. Church Preen
    (also Preen Manor
    under N.G.S.)
11. Caynham
12. Clun
13. Dudelleston
14. Easthope
15. Halford
16. Hope Bagot
17. Kenley
18. Loughton
19. Middleton Scriven
20. Milson
21. Norbury
22. Ratlinghope
23. Ruyton-XI-Towns
24. Sidbury
25. Tasley
26. Uppington
27. Wheathill

● Oaks
1. Acton Round †
2. Lydham Manor *
3. Crowleasowes †
4. Holt Preen *
5. Powis Oak †
6. Frodesley †
7. Nash †
8. Mawley †
9. Lady Oak *†
10. Gospel Oak †
11. Forest Oak *
12. Royal Oak †
13. Princes Oak †
14. Dryton Oak †
15. Admaston Spa †

■ Natives
1. Longnor Hall *
2. Aston-on-Clun †
3. Edgmond †
4. The Quarry †
5. Pitchford Hall *
6. The Hollies †
7. West Felton *
8. Bryneddin Pine †

□ Ornamental or Introduced
1. Longford Grange *†
2. Rowton Castle *†
3. Acton Burnell †
4. Linley Hall *
   † Beech only
5. Walcot Park *

O Notable Collections
1. Apley Castle †
2. Attingham Park †
3. Burford House *
4. Burwarton Hall *
5. Dale End †
6. Halston Hall *
7. Hawkstone Park *
8. Hodnet Hall †
9. Leaton Knolls *
10. Leighton Park *
11. Lilleshall Hall †
12. Loton Park *
13. Netley Hall *
14. Oakly Park *
15. Shavington Park *

* Trees on private land — cannot be visited unless express permission is obtained beforehand.

† Trees can be observed either from road or footpath nearby.
  Many of the parks and gardens containing the trees listed in this book and also other collections of fine trees and shrubs are open on certain summer days under the National Garden Scheme. Details each spring can be obtained from The Gateway, Shrewsbury.

N.G.S. = National Garden Scheme.

Appendix 1
Shropshire Tree Records

In the following lists are notable trees recorded in the county of Shropshire. Most of the information has been supplied by Kim Dodwell of Cruckmeole who has gathered the records together over the past ten years.

Hatton Gardener recorded many trees in the 1940s and his work has been systematically checked where the trees are still standing. When more than one person carries out measurements the recording is open to human error and most records must only be used as a guide. On some trees, for example, the churchyard yews, the measuring is almost impossible due to the unevenness and missing pieces of the trunks. However if a tree is remeasured on the same mark and the bole is smooth, valuable information regarding growth rates and age may be obtained.

The accepted height for measuring girth (circumference) is breast height 1.5 metres (5 feet) from the highest point of the surrounding ground.

If measuring at breast height is impossible then the narrowest point below that mark should be used. Height, where it is recorded, should be measured with a clinometer.

The height and spread of a tree reaches maximum size, then starts to decrease in old age. These features then cannot be measured to give an estimate of age except in young trees. The girth of the trunk though must increase in some way during every year of its life. The age of a tree is thus connected to the circumference alone.

According to Alan Mitchell the mean growth, in girth, of most trees with a full crown is 2.5 cm (one inch) a year. Therefore a tree 2.44 metres (8 feet) in girth is about one hundred years old. Grown in competition it will be about 200 years old and slightly hemmed in about 150 years old. This is of course a very general guide and there are great exceptions at either end of the scale. It must also be remembered that the girth rate slows appreciably the older the tree gets.

Most of the trees in this list are growing on estates, or in parks, gardens and private collections. Many of them are on private land and cannot be visited unless express permission is given by the owner. Certain gardens and parks are open to the public one day a year under the National Gardens Scheme. Details of the Summer openings are usually available in early Spring.

Some notable collections are found in Shropshire, examples being:-

Attingham Park, Oakly Park, Bromfield, Millechope Park Burwarton, Lilleshall Hall, Hodnet Hall, Hawkstone Park, Leaton Knolls and Walcot. Then there are the town trees, particularly around Shrewsbury, and latterly Telford.

Some omissions are bound to occur when trees growing on some private estates and gardens have yet to be visited. We apologise for the omissions but hopefully we have given you a glimpse of the rich tree cover to be found in Shropshire.

SHROPSHIRE RECORDS

CONIFERS

Species & Location	Girth	Other Information	When Measured	Origin	Introduced
MAIDENHAIR TREE *(Ginkgo Biloba)*				China	1758
Bicton Heath House	1.22m (4')		1982		
Netley Hall	1.37m (4'6")		1982		
Valley Hotel,					
Ironbridge	1.40m (4'7")	17m (56') tall.	1984		
YEW *(Taxus Baccata)* See separate list.					
MONKEY PUZZLE *(Auracaria Araucana)*				Chile	1795
Hawkstone Park	2.46m (8'1")				
Pradoe	2.49m (8'2")				
Walcot Park	2.67m (8'9")		1982		
INCENSE CEDAR *(Calocedrus decurrens)*				West U.S.A.	1853
Butler Road,					
Shrewsbury	2.34m (7'8")		1982		
Lilleshall Hall	2.84m (9'4")	25m (82') tall.	1985		
Oakly Park	3.17m (10'5")	28m (92') tall.	1985		
LAWSON'S CYPRESS *(Chamaecyparis lawsoniana)*				West U.S.A.	1854
Lilleshall Hall	2.0m (6'7")	26m (85') tall.	1985		
Millechope Park		29m (98') tallest.	1983		
NOOTKA CYPRESS *(Chamaecyparis Nootkatensis)*				West	1854
Lilleshall Hall	1.93m (6'4")	25m (82') tall.	1985	Canada	
Burwarton Hall	3.12m (10'3")		1982		
MONTEREY CYPRESS *(Cuppressus macrocarpa)*				California	1838
Frodesley					
Churchyard	1.67m (5'6")		1982		
DROOPING JUNIPER *(Juniperus decurva)*				E. Himalayas	1830
Lilleshall Hall	1.14m (3'9")	9m (30') tall.	1985		
PENCIL JUNIPER *(Juniperus virginiana)*				America 1664	
Lilleshall Hall	1.93m (6'4")	12m (40') tall.	1985		
WESTERN RED CEDAR *(Thuja plicata)*				West U.S.A.	1853
Apley Castle	multiple stems	Both these trees	1983		
Preen Manor	multiple stems	are 21m (70') tall			
		and spread over			
		12m (40').	1983		
COAST REDWOOD *(Sequoia sempervirens)*				California	1843
Leaton Knolls	5.03m (16'6")				
Oakly Park	5.66m (18'7")	39m (130') tall.			
Oakly Park	6.10m (20'0")	35m (118') tall.			
Millechope Hall	6.32m (20'9")				
Millechope Hall	7.16m (23'6")	37 (125') tall.			

Species & Location	Girth	Other Information	When Measured	Origin	Introduced
WELLINGTONIA (*Sequoiadendron giganteum*)				California	1853
Leighton Hall	5.40m (17'9")	32m (109') tall.	1984		
Moore Park	5.49m (18')				
Longnor Hall	5.54m (18'2")				
Lilleshall Hall	5.54m (18'2")	29m (98') tall.	1985		
Acton Burnell	5.64m (18'6")		1981		
Burford House	6.10m (20')				
Netley Hall	6.55m (21'6")				
Netley Hall	7.62m (25')				
Oakly Park	8.08m (26'5")	12'. One of line of ten trees. Tallest 42m (138'). Tallest in Shropshire.	1985		
CRYPTOMERIA (*Cryptomeria japonica*)				China	1842
Burwarton Park					
Lilleshall Hall		No measurements			
Acton Burnell					
DAWN REDWOOD (*Metasequoia gyptostroboides*)				China	1941
Hodnet Hall	1.53m (5'0")		1982		
SILVER FIR (*Abies alba*)				Europe	1603
Oakly Park	3.66m (12'0")	43m (141') tall. One of Shropshire's tallest trees.	1985		
GRAND FIR (*Abies grandis*)				Canada	1832
Dale End Park, Ironbridge	2.59m (8'6")	36m (120') tall. Tallest tree in Telford.	1983		
Oakly Park	2.64m (8'8")	38m (128') tall.			
Oakly Park	2.90m (9'6")	41m (135') tall.			
NOBLE FIR (*Abies noblis*)				Oregon	1830
Millechope Park	4.42m (14'6")	39m (130') tall.	1983		
CEDAR OF LEBANON (*Cedrus libani*)				Mt. Lebanon	1638
Pontesford House	3.81m (12'6")				
Millechope Park	4.57m (15')				
Oakly Park	4.98m (16'4")	32m (105') tall.			
Longnor Hall	5.13m (16'10")				
Shelton Hotel	5.26m (17'3")				
Kingsland House	5.49m (18')				
Acton Burnell Castle	5.54m (18'7")				
Marche Manor	6.25m (20'6")		1984		
Burwarton Park	6.40m (21')	18m (60') tall.			
Preen Manor	6.40m (21')		1982		
Walcot Park	7.24m (23'9")	Crown spread of over 18m (60'.)			
Rowton Castle	9.45m (31'0")	One of country's largest and most magnificent cedars. Spread of over 36m (120ft.)	1985		

Species & Location	Girth	Other Information	When Measured	Origin	Introduced
ATLAS CEDAR *(Cedrus atlantica)*				Atlas Mts.	1841
Lilleshall Hall	3.96m (13')	26m (85') tall.	1985		
Netley Hall	3.96m (13')	22m (75') tall.			
Walcot Hall	4.27m (14')		1982		
Netley Hall	4.65m (15'3")	23m (77') tall.	1984		
BLUE ATLAS CEDAR *(Cedrus atlantica glauca)*				Sometimes natural in N. Africa.	1845
Lilleshall Hall	2.92m (9'7")	22m (75') tall.	1985		
DEODAR CEDAR *(Cedrus deodara)*				Himalayas	1831
Longnor Hall	3.91m (12'10")		1984		
Walcot Park	4.27m (14')		1982		
Longnor Hall	4.83m (15'10")	26m (85') tall.	1984		
Lilleshall Hall	5.26m (17'3")	31m (102') tall.	1985		
Burwarton Hall	5.49m (18')		1982		
CHINESE CEDAR *(Cunninghamia lanc)*					
Oakly Park	2.06m (6'9")	23m (76') tall. Rarely found tree.	1985		
LARCH *(Larix decidua)*				Europe	1620
Wellbatch Farm	2.75m (9')		1982		
Hodnet Hall	3.35m (11')		1982		
Netley Hall	3.66m (12')				
Linley Hall	3.66m (12')	One of a group. Reputedly one of the first plantings around 1750. 40m (135') tall.	1984		
Oakly Park	3.86m (12'8")				
Acton Scott	3.92m (12'10")	Standing in woodland.			
Walcot Park	3.96m (13')				
Mawley Hall		No measurements			
MORINDA SPRUCE *(Picea smithiana)*				Asia	1818
Lilleshall Hall	2.67m (8'9")	24m (80') tall. Infrequently found spruce.	1985		
WESTERN HEMLOCK *(Tsuga heterophylla)*				West America	1851
Leaton Knolls	3.05m (10')	32m (108') tall.	1985		
Oakly Park	3.66m (12')				
Burwarton Hall	4.57m (15')				
Oakly Park	4.83m (15'10")	Biggest bole in England	1971		

Species & Location	Girth	Other Information	When Measured	Origin	Introduced
EASTERN HEMLOCK *(Tsuga canadensis)*				East America	1736
Oakly Park	3.66m (12'0")	33m (108') tall.	1985		
"The Deerstalker" (Old Vicarage)					
Wem.	3.71m (12'2")				
Walcot Park	3.58m (11'9")	One of several trees.	1982		
Lilleshall Hall	4.14m (13'7")	Measured at 1'.	1985		
Oakly Park	4.80m (15'9")	23m (77') tall.	1985		
DOUGLAS FIR *(Pseudo tsuga menzieii)*				Brit. Columbia	1827
Millechope Park	3.66m (12')				
Burwarton Hall	3.66m (12')				
Millechope Park	3.81m (12'6")				
Walcot Park	4.72m (15'6")				
Walcot Park	5.44m (17'10")	Clean trunk for 9m (30'). Described as best in England.	1946		
Walcot Park	6.10m (20')	One of the original seedlings 1827.			

The Larches, Linley Hall. Reputedly amongst the first planted in Britain in the 1750s.

Species & Location	Girth	Other Information	When Measured	Origin	Introduced
SUGAR PINE (*Pinus lambertiana*)				West U.S.A.	1827
Hawkstone Hall		Probably the only remaining cone-bearing sugar pine in Britain.			
MONTEREY PINE (*Pinus radiata*)				California	1833
Plaish Hall	(11'2")				
BEACH ORSHORE (*Pinus contorta*)				W. Canada	1855
Oakly Park	1.90m (6'3")	26m (85') tall.	1985		
WESTERN YELLOW PINE (*Pinus ponderosa*)				Rocky Mts.	1828
Burford House	2.06m (6'9")	33m (108') tall.	1982		
Pontesford	2.44m (8')	30m (100') tall.	1982		
Oakly Park	2.87m (9'5")	32m (105') tall.	1985		
Oakly Park	3.43m (11'3')	27m (90') tall.	1985		
JEFFREY'S PINE (*Pinus jeffreyi*)				West U.S.A.	1852
Pitchford Hall	2.44m (8')	Bears huge spined cones.	1982		
Lilleshall Hall	2.61m (8'7")		1985		
BHUTAN PINE (*Pinus Wallichiana*)				Asia	1823
Wenlock Road, Shrewsbury	1.98m (6'6")		1984		
School House, Shrewsbury	2.26m (7'5")		1982		
Lilleshall Hall	2.59m (8'6")	20m (66') tall.			
Kingsland House, Shrewsbury	3.28m (10'9")		1982		
Longnor Hall	3.33m (10'11")	24m (80') tall.	1984		
SCOTS PINE (*Pinus sylvestris*)				Native	
Netley Hall	3.43m (11'3")				
Longnor Hall	3.76m (12'4")				
Netley Hall	3.81m (12'6')				
Millechope Park	3.96m (13'0")		1982		
Longnor Hall	4.95m (16'3")	25m (82') tall.	1984		
AUSTRIAN/CORSICAN PINE (*Pinus nigra*)				Alps	1835
Gains Park	2.90m (9'6")				
Butler Road, Shrewsbury	2.95m (9'8")				
Leaton Knolls	3.05m (10')				
Oakly Park	3.28m (10'9")	36m (118') tall.	1985		
Burwarton Park	3.66m (12')		1985		
Peplow Hall	3.66m (12')				
Oakly Park	4.02m (13'2")	29m (95') tall.	1985		

DECIDUOUS

Species & Location	Girth	Other Information	When Measured	Origin	Introduced
BLACK POPLAR *(Populus nigra (var. betulifolia))*				Native	
Cruckmeole	4.12m (13′6″)	Male 31m (103′) tall.			
Cruckmeole	4.50m (14′9″)	Female 34m (113′) tall.			
Yeaton, Walford Heath	4.27m (14′0″)	22m (75′) tall.			
Pontesbury Hill	4.42m (14′6″)	29m (97′) tall.			
Shawbury	4.57m (15′0″)	18m (60′) tall.			
Shrawardine	4.72m (15′6″)	22m (75′) tall.			
Shrawardine	5.10m (16′9″)	26m (85′) tall.			
Church Stretton (Sandford Avenue)	5.03m (16′6″)	19m (65′) tall.			
Leighton Hall	5.03m (16′6″)	37m (123′) tall. One of country's tallest.			
Oakly Park	5.61m (18′5″)	32m (105′) tall.			
Stapleton	6.40m (21′0″)	30m (100′) tall.			
Longnor Hall	6.10m (20′0″)	38m (124′) tall. Country's tallest.			
Longnor Hall	7.47m (24′6″)	U.K. record girth.			
WHITE POPLAR *(Populus alba)*				Early introduction	
Weston Lullingfields	3.66m (12′0″)				
GREY POPLAR *(Populus canesceus)*				Possibly native	
Marche Manor	2.01m (7′3″)		1984		
Gobowen (Nr. A5)	2.59m (8′6″)	In group of three.	1982		
RAILWAY POPLAR *(Populus nigra)*				Variety of native	
Marche Manor	4.11m (13′6″)	29m (97′) tall.			
Ludlow By-pass	4.42m (14′6″)	37m (122′) tall. Containing mistletoe.	1983		
CRACK WILLOW *(Salix fragilis)*				Native	
Cruckmeole, Yockleton Brook	3.35m (11′0″)	26m (85′) tall.	1984		
WALNUT *(Juglans regia)*				Early introduction	
Netley Hall	3.81m (12′6″)	22m (75′) tall.	1984		
Lydham Manor	3.96m (13′0″)	One of two excellent trees	1982		
Pitchford Village	5.18m (17′0″)	Now gone.	1946		
SILVER BIRCH *(Betula pendula)*				Native	
The Mount, Shrewsbury	2.13m (7′0″)	24m (80′) tall.	1984		

Species & Location	Girth	Other Information	When Measured	Origin	Introduced
COMMON ALDER *(Alnus glutinosa)*				Native	
Cruckmeole	3.05m (10'0")	22m (75') tall.	1984		
Shawbury	3.81m (12'6")		1983		
HORNBEAM *(Carpinus betulus)*				Native	
Shavington Park	2.14m (7'0")				
Lilleshall Hall	2.64m (8'8")		1983		
Burwarton (Old Churchyard)	3.05m (11'6")		1982		
Oakly Park	4.29m (14'1")	27m (90') tall. Spread of 27m (90'). Excellent tree.	1985		
Walcot Park	4.42m (14'6")	Dying back.	1982		
FASTIGIATE HORNBEAM *(Carpinus betulus fastigiata)*				Variety	
Hodnet Hall	1.27m (4'2")				
CUT LEAVED HORNBEAM *(Carpinus betulus 'incisa')*				Rare tree	
The Quarry (nr Swimming Baths)	1.83m (6'0")		1983		
BEECH *(Fagus sylvatica)*				Native	
College Hill, Shrewsbury	3.66m (12'0")				
Hodnet Hall	3.66m (12'0")				
Meole Brace	3.66m (12'0")				
Oakly Park	3.91m (12'10")	35m (115') tall.			
Apley Castle, Telford	4.26m (14'0")				
Burwarton (opp. Church)	4.64m (15'3")	21m (70') tall, 19m (65') spread.	1982		
Burwarton	4.87m (16'0")				
Hawkstone Park (nr 18th Green)	5.51m (18'1")	26m (85') tall, 22m (75') spread.	1985		
FERN LEAVED BEECH *(Fagus sylvactica 'heterophylla')*				Variety of common	1820
Campbells Gdns, Shrewsbury	2.43m (8'0")				
Luciefelde House, Shrewsbury	2.89m (9'6")				
Loton Park	2.97m (9'9")				
Pontesford House	2.97m (9'9")				
Lydham Manor	3.88m (12'9")				
COPPER BEECH *(Fagus sylvatica 'purpurea')*				Europe	before 1700
Apley Castle	2.56m (8'5")				
Lydham Manor	3.05m (11'6")				
Shelton Hotel	3.96m (13'0")				
Millechope Park	3.96m (13'0")				
Burford	4.19m (13'9")				
WEEPING BEECH *(Fagus sylvatica pendula)*				Europe	1820
Hodnet Hall	1.88m (6'2")				
Netley Hall	3.81m (12'6")				

Species & Location	Girth	Other Information	When Measured	Origin	Introduced
SWEET CHESTNUT (*Castanear sativa*)				S. Europe	
Copthorne Hospital	4.49m (14'9")		1982		
Weston under Redcastle	5.61m (18'5")	60% dead 'the Buxtons' field.	1985		
Grinshill	6.29m (20'8")		1981		
Shotton Hall	7.31m (24'0")	27m (90'). Lightning damage	1982		
Kinlet Hall	7.31m (24'0")		1982		
OAK (*Quercus robus/Quercus petraea*)				Native	
Halston	6.24m (20'6")				
Hodnet Hall	6.62/6.65m (21'9"/21'10")	Tennis court/by lake.	1985		
Lilleshall Hall (by Sports Pitch)	6.78m (22'3")				
Loton Park	6.90m (22'10")				
Lilleshall Hall (gardens)	7.01m (23'0")				
Mawley Oak	7.31m (24'0")	27m (90') tall.	1982		
Oakly Park	7.36m (24'2")	31m (103') tall. Excellent oaks on Park.	1985		
Plaish	7.46m (24'6")				
Frodesley Lodge	8.23m (27'0")				
Dryton Oak, Eaton Constantine	8.53m (28'0")				
Acton Round Oak	8.53m (28'0")				
Holt Farm, Plaish	8.83m (29'0")				
Nash Oak	8.83m (29'0")				
Lydham Manor	9.14m (30'0")		1982		
Powis Oak — Underhill Hall	10.36m (34'0")				
Crowleasowes Oak Bitterley	10.97m (36'0")		1983		
Big Oak — Lydham Manor	11.98m (39'4")	One of the country's largest oaks.	1984		
HOLM OAK (*Quercus ilex*)				S. Europe	1500
Lilleshall Hall	2.38m (7'10")				
Kingsland House	2.84m (9'4")				
Pitchford Hall	3.96m (13'0")				
Millechope Park	4.11m (13'6")				
LUCOMBE OAK (*Quercus x hispanica 'Lucombeana'*)				Exeter	1762
Oakly Park	3.09m (10'2")	31m (102'), tallest in Great Britain. One of two.	1985		
Darwin House, Shrewsbury	4.42m (14'6")				
Church Stretton (by Church)	4.87m (16'0")				
Sunniside Gardens, Coalbrookdale	4.87m (16'0")	24m (80') tall, 93' spread. One of the country's largest.			

Species & Location	Girth	Other Information	When Measured	Origin	Introduced
TURKEY OAK *(Quercus cerris)*				S. Europe	1735
Burwarton Park	3.50m (11'6")	19m (65') tall.	1982		
Shavington Park	4.11m (13'6")				
CORK OAK *(Quercus suba)*				S. Europe	1600's
Shavington Park	2.89m (9'6")		1982		
RED OAK *(Quercus borealis)*				E. America	1724
Lilleshall Hall	2.97m (9'9")	26m (85') tall.			
Apley Castle	3.65m (12'0")	60' tall.			
WYCH ELM *(Ulmus glabra)*				Native	
Pulverbatch	3.65m (12'0")	18m (60') tall.			
Shavington Park	5.33m (17'6")				
Apley Castle	5.38m (17'8")	Now gone.			
MULBERRY *(Morus nigra)*				W. Asia	1500
Totterston Hall	1.52m (5'0")				
Sansaw Hall					
College Hill House					
Hadley Village					
Gatacre Park	1.52m (5'0")	Planted in 1932.			
Ludstone					
TULIP TREE *(Liriodendron tulipifera)*				South U.S.A.	1650
Clive House	1.82m (6'0")				
Sheriffhales	2.74m (9'0")				
(Sutherland House)					
Dale End Park,	3.30m (10'10")	26m (86') tall.			
Ironbridge	4.57m (15'0")				
Gatacre Park		24m (80') tall.			
Old Vicarage,					
Highley	5.25m at 0.85m				
LONDON PLANE *(Platanus x hispanica)*				S. France	1650
Burford	3.65m (12'0")	25m (83') tall.			
Millechope Park	3.96m (13'0")	26m (87') tall.			
Wellbatch Farm	3.96m (13'0")	24m (80') tall, 13m (44') spread.	1980		
Oakly Park	3.96m (13'0")	37m (120') tall, tallest in Shropshire.	1985		
Leighton Hall	4.26m (14'0")	31m (103') tall, 13m (45') spread.			
Whitcliffe, Ludlow	4.87m (16'0")				
Burford	4.87m (16")	31m (102') tall.			
St. Mary's Church, Shrewsbury		Two impressive specimens.			
ORIENTAL PLANE *(Platanus orientalis)*				Asia	1550
Hodnet Hall	3.35m (11'0")				
Millechope Park, south of Lake	3.96m (13'0")	31m (100') tall. The finest plane in Britain was found at Weston Park. Top blew			
Millechope Park, east of Lake	3.96m (13'0")	out of tree 1985.			

Species & Location	Girth	Other Information	When Measured	Origin	Introduced
HAWTHORN *(Crataegus monogyna/oxyacantha)*				Native	
Benthall Edge					
Wood	1.37m (4'6")		1982		
Marche Manor	2.13m (7'0")				
COCKSPUR THORN				N. America	1691
A5 Shrewsbury		Excellent			
By-pass		specimens.			
WHITEBEAM *(Sorbus aria)*				Native, many varieties	
A5 Shrewsbury		Excellent			
By-pass		specimens.			
WILD SERVICE TREE *(Sorbus torminalis)*				Native	
Benthall Edge					
Wood	6.86m (2'3")		1982		
Edgmond					
(Robin Road)	1.82m (6'0")		1983		
CRAB APPLE *(Malus sylvestris)*				Native	
		Many large examples in old woodlands.			
GEAN or WILD CHERRY *(Prunus avium)*				Native	
Apley Castle	2.54m (8'4")	19m (65') tall.	1983		
Bromley Hall	2.94m (9'8")	15m (50') tall.	1982		
ROBINIA or FALSE ACACIA *(Robinia pseudoacacia)*				East U.S.A.	1636
Wem "Deerstalker"	4.57m (15'0")				
Old Vicarage					
Acton Round	6.40m (21'0")	22m (75') tall.	1982		
TREE OF HEAVEN *(Ailanthus altissima)*				China	1751
Swan Hill House, Shrewsbury	2.74m (9'0")	Good specimen opposite 'Safeway' frontage, Abbey Foregate. Also Coton Hill.			
Muxton (opp. duck pond)		No measurement.			
HOLLY *(Ilex aquifolium)*				Native	
The largest and oldest are found at "The Hollies", Lords Hill, Snailbeach.		Between 150 and 200 left on the hillside.			
Winsley Hall, Westbury					
Oakly Park, Bromfield	3.12m (10'3")	24m (80') tall, many branched.	1985		

Species & Location	Girth	Other Information	When Measured	Origin	Introduced
SYCAMORE *(Acer pseudoplatanus)*				Roman introduction	
Burwarton	4.57m (15'0")				
Sheriffhales, Southdale House	4.87m (16'0")	45m (150') spread.	1984		
Stottesdon Church	4.87m (16'0")	25m (85') tall.	1983		
Wroxeter Church	5.48m (18'0")				
Halston (by pool)	5.63m (18'6")	48m (160') spread. Biggest spread.			
Halston (in park)	5.79m (19'0")				
Loton Park (by road)	6.70m (22'0")		1980		
Loton Park	6.80m (22'4")		1980		
CAPPADOCIAN MAPLE *(Acer cappadocicum)*				Asia	1838
Lilleshall Hall	1.82m (6'0")	18m (60') tall.	1985		
FIELD MAPLE *(Acer campestre)*				Native	
Shorthill M.R. 433087	1.21m (4'0")				
Crowmeole Lane	2.28m (7'6")				
Shrawardine/Pentre M.R. 374163	2.43m (8'0")	15m (52') tall.			
ITALIAN MAPLE *(Acer opalus)*				S. Europe	1752
Lilleshall Hall	1.95m (6'5")	18m (62') tall.			
SILVER MAPLE *(Acer saccharinum)*				E. America	1725
Lilleshall Hall	2.21m (7'3")	25m (82') tall.			
Church Preen Manor	2.74m (9'0")				
OREGON MAPLE *(Acer macrophylla)*				West U.S.A.	
Oakly Park	3.0m (10'0")	16m (55') tall. Many bunches of mistletoe.	1985		
HORSE CHESTNUT *(Aesculus hippocastanum)*				Albania	1616
Wilcot	5.10m (16'9")	19m (65') tall.	1980		
Uppington Village	5.48m (18'0")				
Longford Grange, Lilleshall	6.47m (21'3")	39m (130') spread, 24m (80') tall. Suckering branches. One of the country's largest.	1985		
PINK HORSE CHESTNUT *(Aesculus x 'carnea')*				Europe	1800's
Lea Cross	1.90m (6'3")	Planted 1937.	1982		

Species & Location	Girth	Other Information	When Measured	Origin	Introduced
LARGE LEAFED LIME *(Tilia platyphyllos)*				Native.	
Hybrid between large leafed and small leafed called Common is usual avenue tree.					
Cheswardine	5.79m (19′0″)		1946		
Great Ness (hedgerow)	6.40m (21′0″)				
Pitchford Hall (with tree house)	7.46m (24′6″)	Country's largest.	1984		
The Quarry		Originals planted 1719 (one was 133′ tall) — they were felled, for safety reasons, 1949.			
SMALL LEAFED LIME *(Tilia cordata)*				Native	
Oakly Park	5.13m (16′10″)	29m (95′) tall. Many other excellent specimens in old woodlands.	1985		
COMMON ASH *(Fraxinus excelsior)*				Native	
Grinshill	4.31m (14′2″)	Records of good specimens sparse.			

Appendix 2
The Future of the Churchyard Yew

On a national basis several researchers are piecing together the history of the yew in Britain. At this stage, firm conclusions cannot be drawn but certain courses of action ought to be taken to protect the ancient churchyard yew.

It is clear that in previous centuries these yews received great reverence. They were as much a part of the churchyard as the church building itself. In certain cases the yew on the site is older that the present church and in Wales, certain yews were actually consecrated.

Although the Victorians tended to romanticise old trees and generally made wild statements about them, they nevertheless cared. Their iron bands, props and cables may have been somewhat misguided, but their attitude of concern towards the churchyard yews must be applauded. These great *living* ancient monuments are now very often no more than dumping grounds for all the unwanted rubbish and paraphernalia of the churchyard. They now shelter anything from weedkiller bottles and oil tanks to dead flowers and broken headstones. It is a tribute to the yew's powers of survival that they live on through this onslaught.

A step in the right direction would be if the local church, parish council, W.I. or other local community association could take on the responsibility for 'looking after' these old trees. In Normandy they are given far greater respect than the British trees.

Advice on any tree surgery required, i.e., pruning off unwanted growth, lessening branch weight, could be made readily available by a network of 'volunteer' professionals who would give their services free if it helped in the protection and public awareness of the churchyard yews.

Shropshire has more ancient yews than any other county in Britain. It is to her advantage to look after these trees that give the county something unique. An added and very important addition to the other natural attractions to be found around the countryside of Shropshire. The ancient and mysterious yews deserve our attention.

SHROPSHIRE'S LARGEST CHURCHYARD YEWS

Name & Map Ref	Sex	Girth	Information
Acton Scott SO 454895	5 trees (2F 3M)	Largest 8.0m (26')	1st rector 1259. Tree closest to church has 'classic' internal stem. Female at corner of churchyard is huge with one dead limb.
Ashford Carbonel SO 525709	5 trees (3F 2M)	Largest 8.2m (27')	Norman church, probable Anglo-Saxon origins. One of the best churchyards to look at ancient yews.
Baschurch SJ 422218	M	5.0m (16.5')	Old churchyard with Saxon connections. Old tree has rotten base, but newer growth flourishes. Iron band once kept the stem together.
Battlefield SJ 513174	1 × M 1 × F	4.2m (13'9") at 1ft. 3.4m (11'0") at 3ft.	Church built after Battle of Shrewsbury 1403. Church built 1410. This churchyard is noticeably unmounded.
Bettws-y-crwyn SO 606814		3.7m (12')	Very tall and clean bole. Lightning damage — Shows on 1790 watercolour.
Billingsley SO 705854	1 × M 1 × F	6.0m (20') 5.5m (18')	Debris in hollow trunk, internal stem bark eaten by goats.
Bishop's Castle SO	M	4.9m (16')	Several trees in churchyard of which this is the largest.
Bucknell SO 355739	2 × F	5.8m (19') 5.5m (18')	Both on south side of church. Pronounced mounding around bases.
Burford SO 583681	M	4.9 (16') (28.2.85)	Extreme south of county, near Tenbury Wells.
Caynham SO 554733	M	5.2m (17') (10.5.84)	At the end of an avenue of younger yews.
Church Preen SO 543982	F	6.8m (22'8")	Shropshire's most famous yew. Completely hollow. Iron band around smooth trunk.
Clun SO 301805	M	Over 10m (Between 33'/35')	Very decayed — north east of churchyard. One of the county's oldest. Other big yews in churchyard. Possible pre-Saxon site.
Dudleston SJ 346385		5.8m (19') (12.2.84)	Several large old yews. Oldest very hollow. Saxon cross in churchyard.
Easthope SO 566952		6.8m (22'3") (20.12.83)	25% of trunk decayed. Circular churchyard of ancient origin. In 1333 patron John Easthope murdered.
Halford SO 436834		5.5m (18')	Churchyard by side of river opposite Craven Arms.

Name & Map Ref	Sex	Girth	Information
Hope Bagot SO 589741	F	7m (23')	Holy well below much decayed yew and spring opposite. Many other trees on nearby footpaths. Norman church.
Kenley SJ 563007		Oldest Unmeasur- able	Several large trees with excellent trunks. One multi-stemmed tree older than rest, probably of great age. Churchyard on high ground. Norman church.
Loughton SO 616831	F	Over 10m (33' at 3') (20.12.83)	Very hollow, with hollow internal stems. Only carbon dated yew in Britain by undedicated Norman chapel dating from 1290. One of the county's major ancient trees.
Middleton Scriven SO 681875	1 × F 1 × M	8.8m (29' at 2ft) (20.12.83) 8.5m (ground)	Mysterious site. Female tree is hollow with internal stem. Male appears solid. Yews in field on opposite side of road from present church.
Milson SO 639728	1 × M	5.9m (19'5") (10.5.84)	South side of Norman church. Hollow tree with much newer growth from trunk.
Norbury SO 364928	M	10.7m (35' at base) (28.12.83)	South side of church. Excellent condition, one of the county's oldest trees. Saxon churchyard. Wall built around tree before 1790s.
Ratlinghope SO 403968	F	5.3m (17'6") (5.1.84)	Clean solid trunk, on the west side of church.
Ruyton-XI-Towns SJ 395223	F	7.7m (25'/26') around remaining pieces.	South east of church. Large trunk has fallen through centre of old shell, many younger stems. Norman church and remains of castle close by, but site is obviously older.
Sidbury SO 685857	M	6.6m (21'9") (30.12.83)	N.N. East of Church. Very decayed at base and hollow. Full of churchyard debris.
Stowe nr. Knighton		6m +	Large spreading yew in remote churchyard.
Tasley SO 697942	F	5.8m (19') at base	Multi-stemmed tree on east of church. Large spreading crown. Church of Norman origins.
Uppington SJ 598094	F	8.7m (28'8") (20.12.83)	Yew south east of church. Huge hollow trunk, measured in 1890s 26'6". Rev. Williams watercolour 1790 shows 2 large trees. Roman altar found on site in late 19th century.
Wheathill SO 623822	2 × M	5.5m & 5.2m (18' & 17')	One in orchard by churchyard.

Appendix 3
Organisations concerned with Trees

Below is a list of organisations who promote tree planting and tree care in the United Kingdom. Advice of new planting schemes are best obtained from local organisations. Grant information can be supplied by the county council and the C.P.R.E. "Men of the Trees" are also concerned with international tree matters.

Arboricultural Association, Ampfield House, Ampfield, Romsey, Hants. SO5 9PA.

British Trust for Conservation Volunteers, 36 St. Mary's Street, Wallingford, Oxon OX10 0EU, also Stirchley Grange, Telford, Shropshire.

Civic Trust, 17 Carlton House Terrace, London SW1Y 5AW.

Council for the Protection of Rural England, 4 Hobart Place, London SW1W 0HY, also Bear Steps, Shrewsbury.

Country Landowners Association, 16 Belgrave Square, London SW1X 1PQ.

Countryside Commission, John Dower House, Crescent Place, Cheltenham.

Forestry Commission, Marches Office, Whitcliffe, Ludlow, Shropshire.

Men of the Trees, Crawley Down, Crawley, Sussex RH10 4HL, also 23 Aysgarth Road, Shrewsbury.

National Farmers Union, Agriculture House, Knightsbridge, London SW1X 7NJ, also Agriculture House, Barker Street, Shrewsbury.

Nature Conservancy Council, Attingham Park, Atcham, Shropshire.

Shropshire County Council, Planning Department, Shirehall, Shrewsbury.

Shropshire Trust for Nature Conservation, Agriculture House, Barker Street, Shrewsbury.

The Tree Council, 35 Belgrave Square, London SW1X 8QN.

The Woodland Trust, Grantham, Lincolnshire.

The Green Wood Trust, Rose Cottage, Coalbrookdale, Ironbridge, Shropshire.

Acknowledgements

Barbara Bates, Terina Jones, Mary Wright, Elizabeth Powell, Barbara Morton, Tom Beardsley, Frank Jones, Dr. Switsur, Alan Meredith, Alan Mitchell, H. G. D. Foxall, Col. Faithful, Earl of Plymouth, Mr. Windsor Clive, Staff of Local Studies Library, Shrewsbury, Col. Sykes, Mr. & Mrs. Colthurst, Mr. & Mrs. Parish, Kim Dodwell, Mr. & Mrs. Trevor Jones, Mr. L. Berry, Sir M. Leighton, Sir J. More, A. V. Nicholson, Audrey Ashwell, Mr. Parkinson, G. Adams, Walter Williams, Peter Jackson, J. Treasure, Lord Boyne, Mr. C. Bridgeman, Mrs. J. Esum, John Sugden, C. Holland, D. Griffiths, Rex Cartwright, Eric Wiggins, Harry Synge, Shropshire County Library Service, Mr. Heber-Percy, Department of Environment and the numerous other people who gave information and help for this publication. I am greatly indebted to Alan Howard for his work on the Tree Mythology chapter and his general interest and encouragement on the publication. Also Tom Foxall who has driven many miles around the county looking for good photographs and Kim Dodwell for all the information he supplied.

Bibliography

The Common Ground, Richard Mabey
Trees in the Wild, Gerald Wilkinson
The Golden Bough, Sir James Frazer
The Churchyard Yew and Immortality, Vaughan Cornish
Yew Trees in Great Britain and Ireland, John Lowe
The Oxford Book of Trees, B. E. Nicholson & A. R. Clapham
Trees of Britain & N. Europe, Alan Mitchell
Shropshire Field Names, H. G. D. Foxall
Churches of Shropshire, Watercolours — Rev. Williams
History of Shropshire, Barry Trinder
The Shropshire Landscape, Trevor Rowley
Nooks & Corners of Shropshire, H. Thornhill-Timmins
Ludlow Town & Neighbourhood, Oliver Baker
Celtic Britain, L. Laing
Origins of Britain, L. Laing & J. Laing
Pagan Celtic Britain, Anne Ross
Trees & Woodlands in the British Landscape, Oliver Rackham
Landscape with Trees, Miles Hadfield
The Natural History of an English Forest, Norman Hickin
The Great Yew Forest, Richard Williamson
History of Claverley, W. H. Dawkes
Man, Myth and Magic, S. G. F. Brandon
Man, Myth and Magic, A. J. Huxley
Trees of Britain in History and Legend, G. H. Wilkes